The Immemorial

THE ITALIAN LIST

ALSO FROM THE ITALIAN LIST

Edited by ALBERTO TOSCANO

Class
ANDREA CAVALLETTI
Translated by Elisa Fiaccadori

The Labour of Spirit
MASSIMO CACCIARI
Translated by Matteo Mandarini

Self-Portrait in the Studio
GIORGIO AGAMBEN
Translated by Kevin Attell

Name and Image
GIANNI CARCHIA
Translated by Matteo Mandarini

The Twilight of Politics
MARIO TRONTI
Translated by Matteo Mandarini

As Cruel as Anyone Else
ANGELO DEL BOCA
Translated by Richard Braude

Feminism in Revolt
CARLA LONZI
Edited by Luisa Lorenza Corna and
Jamila M. H. Mascat

The World Machine
PAOLO VOLPONI
Translated by Richard Dixon

The Soul of Brutes
CARLO GINZBURG

The Idea of World
PAOLO VIRNO
Translated by Lorenzo Chiesa

Primo Levi
MARCO BELPOLITI
Translated by Clarissa Botsford

This Body That Inhabits Me
ROSSANA ROSSANDA
Translated by Richard Braude
Edited by Lea Melandri

The Golden Horde
Edited by NANNI BALESTRINI by
PRIMO MORONI
Translated by Richard Braude

The Writer and the People
ALBERTO ASOR ROSA
Translated by Matteo Mandarini

Andrea Cavalletti

THE IMMEMORIAL

The Subject and Its Doubles

TRANSLATED BY MAX MATUKHIN

LONDON NEW YORK CALCUTTA

This book has been translated thanks to a translation grant awarded by the Italian Ministry of Foreign Affairs and International Cooperation.

Questo libro è stato tradotto grazie a un contributo alla traduzione assegnato dal Ministero degli Affari Esteri e della Cooperazione Internazionale italiano.

Seagull Books, 2025

First published in Italian as
L'immemorabile: Il soggetto e i suoi doppi

This edition has been published in agreement with
Neri Pozza Editore through the MalaTesta Literary Agency, Milan

First published in English translation by Seagull Books, 2025

Paperback ISBN 978 1 80309 529 5

Hardback ISBN 978 1 80309 528 8

British Library Cataloguing-in-Publication Data
A catalogue record for this book is available from the British Library

Typeset by Seagull Books, Calcutta, India

What really matters about the past is what we cannot remember. The rest, what memory conserves or retrieves, is mere sediment.

—Furio Jesi

Contents

I

In Vienna, during the First Days of 1825 . . .

1. During the first days of 1825, a young man by the name of Meyer is making the news in Vienna. He is 14 years old, of a scrofulous constitution, still has a boy's voice and does not fancy studying. On 17 January, all of a sudden and without any clear cause, he falls into a deep sleep. His parents immediately notify the doctor, who, after a careful visit, prescribes a bath, the application of leaches to his head and mercuric chloride. A spasm, a sort of trismus, grips the sleeping body: the boy's mouth is now closed shut, and it becomes impossible to make him swallow the concoction. 'Better to die than to drink that nasty medicine . . . ' The next day, however, Meyer wakes up healthy as a horse, behaving as if nothing had happened, claims to have slept well and eats with good appetite. And then sinks back into his sleep.

Things proceed in this manner for a few weeks. Then sleep gives way to delirium. Although his eyelids remain shut, the young man now displays a great vivacity and expresses the most ardent of desires: he asks to be driven in a carriage, to ride on horseback, to dance. In his singular somnambulism, he can, in fact, dedicate himself to these activities without the slightest difficulty. Moreover, he can answer questions without a hitch and, although one never sees him open his eyes, he reads, writes or, preferably, plays cards while announcing the next relapse to his doctors and discussing with them the effects of their medicine. Once the crisis has passed, Meyer has no recollection of it, nor does he display any traces of it.

No less of a celebrity than Joseph Frank—the famous pathologist from the University of Vilnius, the philanthropist who served as an inspiration for Honoré de Balzac's Dr Benassis—examines the case and excludes any possibility of fraud. But then how is one to define the bizarre phenomenon? The professor replies with assurance to the inevitable question—what would you have called it if Meyer's eyes had stayed open? Temporary delirium, obviously. Excellent, well then let's keep to that diagnosis, since the eyelids' spasm does not change the state of things in any way: indeed, we are dealing with a case of 'periodic mental alienation'.[1]

2. Twenty years later, on a dark December night, obeying a mysterious convocation written in an esoteric language, Théophile Gautier arrives on the Île Saint-Louis, 'espèce de oasis de solitude au milieu de Paris' (an oasis of solitude in the midst of Paris); he crosses the threshold of the Hôtel Pimodan, timidly goes up the sumptuous staircase by Louis Le Vau in his old tuxedo and is enthusiastically welcomed by the other guests and by the doctor hosting the evening, who immediately offers him a little plate with a greenish pâté. He then sits down at the laden dinner table to enjoy a meal exquisite and bizarre in equal measure: by now, he has abandoned himself 'without resistance to the effects of the fantastical drug', and even the caustic concoction becomes like sugar for him, just as the water transforms into wine, meat into raspberries and the other guests change shape and appear in supernatural colours.

'Hallucination, that strange guest, had taken up residence in me,' Gautier will go on to remember. 'Personal experience is the *criterium* of truth,' asserts for his part Moreau de Tours. Before founding the Club des Hachischins, the doctor had done his research while travelling at length in the Orient, and in Paris he repeated his experiments on numerous occasions. He can therefore speak in the first person: he collects his

1 Joseph Frank, *Traité de pathologie interne*, VOL. 2 (Brussels: Société Encyclographique, 1842), p. 37n2.

scrupulous observations, confronts them with other opinions and testimonials, and then, defying the incredulity of his colleagues, transforms his ideas into a book dedicated to his teacher Jean-Étienne Dominique Esquirol. *Du hachisch et de l'aliénation mentale: Études psychologiques* appears in 1845 and soon becomes a minor classic and consequently a rarity for bibliophiles.[2] In the eyes of Moreau, alienation is 'a distinct mode of existence', a sort of interior life which has recourse to elements and materials from 'real or positive life', of which it is merely a reflection or an internal echo. Its most typical and complete psychological manifestation is the state of dreaming. Of course, even before this organicist principle had been clearly formulated, the old analogy between the two conditions had piqued the interest of doctors such as William Cullen and Pierre-Jean-Georges Cabanis on the one hand and philosophers such as Maine de Biran on the other. Still in 1845, Frédéric Dubois d'Amiens combined the two interpretations, defending the importance of philosophy before his colleagues at the Académie nationale de médecine. He vaguely evoked Biran's theses, adapting them to his own eclecticism: if, in a dream state, the soul remains awake in the sleeping body, insanity, for Dubois, was the sleep of thought in a body that was awake or even overexcited. 'Now, in every way dreams imitate insanity,'[3] one would go on to read 40 years later in a salient section of *Matière et mémoire*: here, mimeticism confuses dreaming and insanity, well after René Descartes and well before any discussions concerning whether insanity in Descartes is distinct from the oneiric state—so that doubt or the *cogito* would exclude folly (Michel Foucault)—or is merely overlooked—and the one who dreams is in fact 'madder than the madman' (Jacques Derrida).[4]

---

2 Jacques-Joseph Moreau (Moreau de Tours), *Hashish and Mental Illness* (Hélène Peters and Gabriel G. Nahas eds, Gordon J. Barnett trans.) (New York: Raven Press, 1973).

3 Henri Bergson, *Matter and Memory* (N. M. Paul and W. S. Palmer trans) (New York, NY: Zone Books, 1991), p. 228.

4 Jacques Derrida, 'Cogito and the History of Madness' in *Writing and Difference* (Alan Bass trans.) (Chicago, IL: Chicago University Press, 1978), p. 51.

Henri Bergson read *Du hachisch*. But certainly Moureau's thesis—which was as well known as it was radical—was beyond any comparison or similitude: it is not that there is a relation between dreaming and insanity, there is an indistinction, 'rêves et délire se confondent à leur origine' (dreams and delirium conflate at their origin). Hence, if the greenish pâté transforms any food into another, this confusion is so profound as to be able to transform, in a no less amazing way, any food into a hallucinogenic pâté. A decade had passed since Charles Laségue, in a rare move, at the apogee of organicist theory, separated dreams from insanity, assigning only to the former the phenomena and visions produced by magnetism, drugs or liquors, when Benjamin Ball (who was in fact an admirer of his) recounted an instructive memory to his students:

> My teacher Moreau (de Tours) often told me that when he began working at the Salpêtrière, he had the idea of testing the effects of hashish on the hysterics in his ward, with surprising results. Gripped by a reasonable sense of scruple, he suddenly substituted the [hashish] pills that he usually administered with pellets of bread: he was mortified to observe that the same symptoms reproduced themselves and with even greater intensity.[5]

3. Do not trust stopwatches, the writer warns. For him, 15 minutes had lasted three centuries. And the doctor adds that, one evening, during one of his first experiments with hashish, it had taken him many hours to walk a mere few steps along the Passage de l'Opéra. To him, the long gallery full of mirrors seemed like a dilated theory of vague and vibrant signs, while, up above, the geometry of the skylight flowed slowly along the line of the mouldings, allowing midday rays or else uncertain lunar ones to filter through. Time is the accident of accidents, Epicureans used to say. Time itself, the measure or 'la poésie du temps, avec ses illusions' (the poetry of time, with its illusions), as Jean-Marie Guyau would go on to say one day against Immanuel Kant, is nothing other than an

5 Benjamin Ball, *Leçons sur les maladies mentales* (Paris: Asselin et Houzeau, 1890), p. 641.

effect of perspective and, above all, 'de perspective spatiale représentée à l'imagination' (of spatial perspective represented to the imagination).[6] The time effect changes with the change of the focus and the distance of the projection, exposed like an optical sensation to the distortions of madness, to the troubles of hallucinations. 'Time only exists in relation to the succession of our thoughts,' writes Moreau de Tours. In 1855, he returns to his now-famous book, responding to criticisms and clarifying his positions in a long essay. He had taken his first truth from popular wisdom: 'La folie est le rêve de l'homme éveillé' (Madness is the wakeful man's dream)—and the science of his contemporaries had rejected it. But truth is an open battle, and allies can come from far afield. Moreau then cites Baruch Spinoza: 'error, as will be clear at once, is dreaming whilst one is awake, and if this is very evident it is called madness.'[7] So what would happen, the doctor asks himself, if an individual regained their reason after 15 or even 30 years?

> Exactly the same thing as would have happened if they had woken up after a few hours of sleep: they would be surprised to not find everything as it was when they were gripped by madness. Their eyes would seek out the same objects, their affects would seek out the same people . . . They would have great difficulty in recognizing their own children in the adults before them, and they would even doubt themselves: where do these wrinkles come from, and these whitened hairs, all of these signs of ageing?[8]

---

6 Jean-Marie Guyau, *La genèse de l'idée de temps* (Alfred Fouillée intro.) (Paris: Alcan, 1890), p. 106; Henri Bergson, 'Compte rendue de *La Genèse de l'idée de temps* de J.-M. Guyau' in *Écrits philosophiques* (Arnaud Bouaniche, François, Élie During, Frédéric Fruteau de Laclos, Frédéric Keck, Stéphane Madelrieux, Camille Riquier, Ghislain Waterlot and Frédéric Worms eds) (Paris: Presses Universitaires de France, 2001[1891]), pp. 148–49.

7 Baruch Spinoza, *Treatise on the Correction of the Intellect* in *Ethics and Treatise on the Correction of the Intellect* (Andrew Boyle trans.) (London: J. M. Dent., 1993), §65 (p. 243n); Jacques-Joseph Moreau de Tours, 'De l'identité de l'état de rêve et de la folie', *Annales médico-psychologiques* 3(1) (1855): 386.

8 Moreau de Tours, 'De l'identité de l'état de rêve et de la folie': 393.

Every alienist has been a witness to similar resurrections, because—much like sleep—insanity divides life into two. Or rather, those who sleep or are delirious penetrate into a separate world, they gain access to a new, independent existence, which supplants the former one and replaces it. Thus, the illness multiplies the lives of the alienated individual, just as it transforms and duplicates their personality. And the transformation must be complete, since the 'I' is one rather than many, since the body cannot move simultaneously in two opposite directions, since the mind affirms or denies, and it cannot deny without ceasing to affirm, nor can it be subject to two transformations or live simultaneously in ways that would be mutually exclusive: 'Either one can reason or one cannot, either one is mad or one isn't, one cannot be half-mad, or three-quarters mad, or only mad en-face or in profile.'[9]

Wherever the 'I' is identical to itself, personalities (unlike foodstuffs) multiply but do not blend. And the borders between them could not be any clearer: memory, Moreau says, renews interrupted relations without filling in the void that has now been opened up in existence. The 'I' is one, and its life must at the very least be split into two: it will at times be wakeful, at others asleep, lucid or dreamy, rational or mad. The partition between the normal and the pathological harkens back here to the disjunction between wakefulness (activity) and sleep (passivity), and reflects it by establishing a coherent order of values. Here, where these stages follow each other without coalescing, asymmetry reigns, and a hierarchy is now firmly established. If one therefore switches completely from one life to another it is because one life—delirious or ecstatic, subject to folly or stimulants—is merely a lacuna of the other, its time merely a suspension of the other's.

Here, where the 'I' is one, both an alternative and an order find themselves imposed: existence will always be 'first' or 'second' and therefore active or passive, true and healthy or sick and parasitic, profound and essential or conventional, faithful to itself or mutable.

9 Moreau de Tours, 'De l'identité de l'état de rêve et de la folie': 403.

Here, around the table in the salon of the Hôtel Pimodan, the one cannot help but multiply and the many cannot help but follow one another and crowd into one: every guest occupies his place while he executes or undergoes the strangest of metamorphoses, and it is as if the voices of the empiricist, the spiritualist and the criticist—of those who admit only a multiplicity of psychological states and those who recognize the unalterable unity of the 'I', both in terms of sensation and of intellectual intuition—alternated and merged in him.

4. Frank tells the story of the young Meyer, who lives with his eyes closed.[10] Moreau draws attention to the case—borrowed from Philippe Pinel—of a priest tormented by the worst of nightmares: he dreams that his closest friends conspire against him, and he can feel them approaching, ready to kill him, he sees his killers multiply, he believes himself to be the target of their mortal blows, and while he dreams and suffers *his eyes are open*, he listens to the sound of the church bells and counts the hours of the night. External conditions can indeed change from sleep to wakefulness, Moreau writes, but the dream can continue, overstepping one state to invade another, to turn into delirium.

In October of 1858, Étienne Eugène Azam, a surgeon in Bordeaux, the son of an alienist and a psychology enthusiast himself, meets Félida X. Born in 1843, the girl has been suffering for several months from a strange transformation: her personality changes so rapidly and intensely that one could reasonably wonder whether she lives two distinct lives. With these words, on 20 May 1876, Azam will present the case to the Académie des sciences morales, immediately clarifying that Félida does not actually possess a 'double consciousness', she does not believe she has been transformed into someone else, like William Benjamin Carpenter's patient, who thought she had become an old priest.[11] Under the influence of Victor Egger—the philosopher admired by Bergson—

10 Frank, *Traité de pathologie interne*, VOL. 2, p. 65n1.

11 Étienne Eugène Azam, 'Amnésie périodique, ou doublement de la vie', *Revue scientifique* 2(5) (1876): 486.

Azam will go on to correct his diagnosis on more than one occasion. First, by recognizing the phenomenon of personality doubling, then of the double personality, and finally even going so far as to contradict himself (arguing that it is not the personality but the consciousness of the patient that is double). 'I', 'person', 'character', 'consciousness' and 'personality' were, for that matter, merely precarious signs in a little-explored land at the time, still jumbled in a web of synonymies. But in 1887, Azam collects for the first time the studies on Félida in the now-classic *Hypnotisme, double conscience et altérations de la personnalité*. And, while writing the preface, Jean-Martin Charcot recruits both the doctor and the patient to the École de la Salpêtrière, declaring that both the subject and the nature of the phenomena belong to the category of hysterical hypnosis.

Certainly, as far as hysteria went, Azam did not have any doubts. Just as he did not harbour any doubts regarding Félida's amnesia. He attributes it to a defect in her blood flow, which, according to him, only reached one of the young woman's cerebral hemispheres, throwing her into a strange condition of '*total* somnambulism'. Never, in fact, had he seen such a perfect somnambulist, entirely capable of thought, who is not asleep at all and is therefore hypnotizable, as if she were in a normal state of wakefulness. The 'second' phase has established itself in her, dominating the entirety of her vital functions and in fact giving her a heretofore unknown energy. And now the young woman lives a new and even richer existence. Or would it be more accurate to say that she has a new personality? Or perhaps a new consciousness? While his teacher is introducing Azam's book, Georges Gilles de la Tourette dedicates a chapter to Félida in his *L'hypnotisme et les états analogues au point de vue médico-légal* and responds with trained assurance:

> When the attacks are prolonged enough, the somnambulist seems to possess a double life, so to speak, for the simple reason that he alternately finds himself immersed in two states—one normal and the other pathological. Upon awakening, oblivion reigns, and this suffices for the two phases to be distinguishable. There is therefore a true double life, even more so than a *double-*

> *ment* of personality, a term coined by mental medicine and which is inappropriate in this circumstance.[12]

But the question remains open, at least until its twentieth-century echo: 'What psychoanalysis considers to be an unconscious,' observes Gilbert Simondon,

> should in fact be considered a counter-ego, a double that is not a true ego, since it is never endowed with actuality; it can only be expressed in dreams or automatic acts, not in the state of integrated activity. Janet's idea of the personality splitting is perhaps closer to reality than that of the unconscious, which has been accepted since Freud. However, it would be more appropriate to speak of a *doubling* [*doublement*] of personality, of a phantom-personality, than of a splitting [*dédoublement*] of personality. What splits is not the actual personality, but another personality, a personality equivalent that is constituted outside the field of the ego, like a virtual image is constituted beyond a mirror for the observer without ever really being there. If there were a veritable splitting of the personality, one could not speak of a first state and a second state; even if the second state occupies a time frame longer than the first state, it does not have the same structure and can be recognized as the second state.[13]

Thus, Simondon corrects Sigmund Freud by retracing Pierre Janet's steps, and corrects Janet, thus eventually finding himself not too far off from Gilles de la Tourette, as if he too had travelled along the *rampe admirable* alongside Gautier, to be welcomed a century later (do not place any faith in stopwatches and calendars) in Moreau de Tours's strange club. *C'est lui! C'est lui!—a* strange chorus of voices seems to greet him, like that day—*qu'on lui donne sa part* [give him his slice]! Wherever there is individuation, even understood in Simondon's terms as a combined process,

12 Georges Gilles de la Tourette, *L'hypnotisme et les états analogues au point de vue médico-légal* (Paul Brouardel pref.) (Paris: E. Plon, 1887), p. 245.

13 Gilbert Simondon, *Individuation in Light of Notions of Form and Information* (Taylor Adkins trans.) (Minneapolis: University of Minnesota Press, 2020), p. 321.

as a continuous birth, as the succession of 'metastable equilibria', there suspension, doubling and hierarchy still reign. It is precisely when 'vivre est perpétuer une permanente naissance relative' (living means perpetuating a permanent relative birth) that the one does not cease to be two, the first cannot stop doubling, while the real separates from the virtual, and the true personality from its pathological reflection.

5. Like the young Meyer, like Janet's later patient—the famous Léonie—Félida retains no memory of her attacks. Or rather, in her normal life she forgets the other, while in the latter she remembers the former. Thus, wherever a lacuna appears, continuity affirms its predominance. But is it enough for a life to be incapable of being remembered for it to be considered as healthy? And is that which presents itself as empty truly lacking? 'Normal' and 'first' do not have an absolute value, Azam would respond, but merely a relative one with respect to the illness:

> By calling one of Félida's state 'normal', I did not mean 'a state of perfect health'. I merely called it that by comparison with the other one and for lack of a better term. But in fact neither of the two states is normal; for, as I have explained, Félida is hysterical [. . .] I therefore do not have any difficulty in admitting that both states are morbid, all while maintaining that one of the two—and for lack of a better term I call it normal—has a greater resemblance to her earlier life, which is entirely unknown and has never been perfectly healthy, despite not causing any worries in the people close to Félida.[14]

This response confirms, however, that the regulating principle is that of an imagined anteriority, of an original and in turn un-rememberable continuity. The normal condition is the one that the doctor presupposes, that Félida cannot recall (even under hypnosis) and that her loved ones have never known (being unable to distinguish her from the person

14 Étienne Eugène Azam, *Hypnotisme, double conscience et altérations de la personnalité* (J.-M. Charcot pref. and Serge Nicholas intro.) (Paris: L'Harmattan, 2004[1887]), p. 126.

who did not unsettle them, despite already being affected by the illness). The normal condition is the one that has never made an appearance; if not, one might say, as a negative, in its most obscure projection. Indeed, at times during her adolescence, Félida experienced a special state of sudden and intense agitation, which threw her into a panic and took her breath away. She then found herself immersed in the purest and most total alienation and upon not seeing any familiar faces or object around her, she could only yell, 'I'm afraid! . . . I'm afraid!' Gradually, with time, these attacks would go on to disappear, leaving in their stead, around the age of 30, a simple alternation. It is only then that Félida's life story could unfold—seen 'from above', as Azam writes—in its proper chronology: from the normal phase of the personality that she had from birth to the life doubled by amnesia and finally to the third phase, 'nouvelle et différente par son intégrité [new and different due to its oneness]'. It is only when seen from this perspective that the phenomenon achieved the orderly regularity of a biographical development: the periods of attacks and recovery, the memories and amnesias, the continuities and the temporal suspensions could succeed one another . . . thereby confirming that everything in psychology is an 'effet de la perspective' (effect of perspective). Thus, the young Meyer announced with his eyes closed the progression of the illness to his doctors, all while ironically indicating to them the proper observation point. It was the position of the 'I' and at the same time the object of its aim, the point in which the author and the subject, reality and biography overlap, and in which everything unites and divides, belonging both to the observer and to the observed, mine and already not mine. Psychologists, Bergson would go on to say, search for the 'I' and insist on finding it in psychological states, but the variety of the latter has been obtained 'by transporting oneself outside the 'I' altogether, so as to make a series of sketches, notes, and more or less symbolic and schematic diagrams.'[15]

15 Henri Bergson, *An Introduction to Metaphysics* (T. E. Hulme trans., John Mullarkey and Michael Kolkman eds) (New York: Macmillan, 1985), pp. 193–94; translation modified.

It seems like the young Meyer, with his periodic alienations, and like him the second Félida reach the point of separation from which alone a unity of the subject could be constituted. This is, perhaps, the position of the current 'I' which (in a schematic, fragmentary or symbolic manner) recalls the past, makes it its own and ties itself to it. Perhaps in Meyer and in Félida (and thus in everyone under the spell of greenish potions) the common structure of the subject breaks up and becomes exposed; perhaps people live confessing through their most common gestures and betraying in every word that the memory of the self demands an un-rememberable self, that individual identity implies a scission and lacuna, that presence is the promise of its crisis and that the pulsating centre of consciousness is empty. If a secondary or insane I myself can always take my place it is because I am already split in sleep, because only a doubleness restores unity, it is only in division that biographic continuity is welded together and maintained . . .

II

The 'Fundamental Sense'

6. 'Insofar as I can affirm that I have all of a sudden become someone else [. . .] as much as a personality may split, all of these scissions come about as the scission of an identical egoic pole which endures in them', Edmund Husserl would go on to write in 1931.[1] More than half a century earlier, in 1876, the *Revue scientifique* had published Paul Janet's response to the invitation of its director, Émile Algave: 'My dear friend, you asked me for an article on Azam's rather curious contribution [. . .] I do not believe, however, that this case presents greater difficulties than those of sleep and somnambulism, of which it merely represents a very striking development.' And if, in one case or in the other, the 'I' can seem double—the philosopher continued—one must ask oneself, what does its unity consist of? It is in fact very different to say 'I am I' or 'I am such an I', 'I am' or 'I am Peter or Paul'.

> When Descartes says *Cogito ergo sum* he does not add *sum Cartesius*. Whether he is Descartes or someone else interests him little, since it is his pure existence that he is affirming and nothing else. Now [. . .] I may forget my own name, my age, my place of residence, without however ceasing to be me.[2]

1 Edmund Husserl, *Zur Phänomenologie der Intersubjektivität. Texte aus dem Nachlass*, VOL. 3: *1929–1935*, Husserliana, VOL. 15 (Iso Kern ed.) (The Hague: Njihoff, 1973), p. 254.

2 Paul Janet, 'La notion de personnalité', *Revue scientifique*, 2nd EDN, 10(50) (1876): 574.

Janet thus distinguished (thereby remaining faithful in a way to Maine de Biran) the *sense of individuality* from the *fundamental sense of existence*: the former concerns the external profile of the subject, whereas the latter concerns the fundamental 'I'. If the sense of individuality, which determines but does not constitute the fundamental 'I', can disappear or remain in the shadows, or else fall under the influence of confusion and deceit (the legal *error in persona*), nothing by contrasty could ever perturb the sense of pure existence. With a thesis that Bergson will go on to take up in his own way, he argues that life may appear double, at least externally, while essentially remaining one. And it is precisely 'from pure existence that psychologists should proceed when they speak of the unity and identity of the "I"'. These ideas, Janet concluded, would certainly need developing . . .

7. Denying the novelty of the *dédoublement* and tracing it back to the general phenomenon of somnambulism, the spiritualist Janet minimized the importance of Félida's case, all while restoring to it a philosophical tenor which was still evident to Biran, to Georg Wilhelm Friedrich Hegel or to Arthur Schopenhauer, situating it at the centre of the modern problematic of the subject by demonstrating its clear Cartesian origin. In fact, one could remark that he thus revealed, with the most calibrated and felicitous of words, a difficulty that would become a battleground among the greatest interpreters of the twentieth century, which goes back to the transition from the *cogito* to the *sum*—or to the 'insidious *ergo* [*verfängliche* "*ergo*"]'[3]—and is therefore inseparable from the more classic, though never fully resolved difficulties, of the Cartesian substantialization of thought and of the nature (syllogistic or otherwise) of the *cogito ergo sum*.

One may think back to the disagreement between the interpretations of Ferdinand Alquié and Martial Guéroult, a late Cartesian battle that

3 Martin Heidegger, *Nihilism* (Frank A. Capuzzi trans., David Farrell Krell ed.), Nietzsche, VOL. 4 (San Francisco, CA: Harper & Row, 1979), p. 113.

goes back to the canonical readings of Étienne Gilson and Léon Brunschvicg and one that is in certain ways prolonged in the no less difficult but more explicit and better-known dispute between Michel Foucault and Jacques Derrida (who will also go on to quote Guéroult against his adversary), later taken up in turn by Jean-Luc Nancy without Foucault's giving any impression of having noticed it.[4] In 1955, when Guéroult's great work, *Descartes selon l'ordre des raisons*, had already been out for two years, Alquié inaugurated his course at the Sorbonne, entitled *Science et métaphysique chez Descartes*, by asking the question directly: why are the *cogito* and the *sum* in the first person? To give an answer, he told the auditorium, one had to tackle Descartes's texts directly and first and foremost his answers to Gassendi, forgoing an examination of the contemporary discussion, which he hardly even mentioned, quickly citing, in addition to the pages penned by Guéroult (the essay 'Le Cogito et la notion "pour penser il faut être"' was moreover from 1937), the canonical texts by Henri Gouhier and the recent study by Ginette Dreyfus.[5] The decision was a polemical one, and in fact Alquié immediately indicated his chosen targets:

> Why are the *cogito* and the *sum* in the first person? How does Descartes know that what he thinks is him? Why, instead of saying 'there is thought' or 'one thinks' or even 'a being thinks' [. . .] does he say: *sum*, 'this being is me'? Brunschvicg [. . .] was particularly scandalized by this first-person *cogito*, and would have wanted Descartes to say: 'I doubt, therefore God is', he would have wanted him to immediately shift from doubt to a universal, impersonal thought.[6]

4 Jean-Luc Nancy, *Ego sum*: *Corpus*, *Anima*, *Fabula* (Marie-Eve Morin trans.) (New York, NY: Fordham University Press, 2016).

5 Ginette Dreyfus, 'Discussion sur le "Cogito" et l'axiome "Pour penser il faut être"', *Revue Internationale de Philosophie* 6(19) (1952): 117–25.

6 Ferdinand Alquié, *Leçons sur Descartes*: *Science et métaphysique chez Descartes* (Paris: La Table Ronde, 2005), p. 152.

Thus, by placing Brunschvicg in his sights, Alquié could hit his source, who, for that matter, was a well-known target for his audience. The work in question was indeed the fundamental *Commentaire* to the *Discours de la méthode* (1925) which had earned Gilson in 1929 public praise from Husserl: '. . . we know through recent researches—particularly the fine and penetrating work of Messrs Gilson and Koyré—that a great deal of Scholasticism is hidden in Descartes' meditations as unarticulated prejudice.'[7] Indeed, in that early work, after having recalled the 'Sum, ergo Deus est' from the *Regulae ad directionem ingenii*, the great historian of philosophy observed that in essence the text of the *Discours* seems to only 'ascertain' that the intuition of personal existence and that of divine existence 'mutually imply each other, bringing about a deduction whose formulation could be: *Dubito, ergo Deus est*.'[8] Beginning with the famous 1937 monograph entitled *René Descartes*, Brunschvicg will go on to cite on numerous occasions this 'formule concentrée' (condensed formula), so coherent with his interpretation of the cartesian *moi* as the 'sujet d'une pensée universelle' (subject of a universal thought), and therefore with a critique of the subjectivist and solipsistic reading and the conception of the *cogito* as the synthetic intuition that unites the existence of the 'I' with that of God, or better yet, which 'avant d'être l'intuition du moi [. . .] est l'intuition de Dieu' (before being an intuition of the I . . . is the intuition of God).[9] Basing himself on the Cartesian idea of the infinite 'in action', Brunschvicg defines both divine nature and the nature of thought with a single gesture: 'The God of Descartes is not above the heavens but in the deepest depths of man, *immediate* like the *Cogito*, or rather *immanent* to the *Cogito*.'[10] It is only if divinity possesses the same

7 Edmund Husserl, *The Paris Lectures* (Peter Koestenbaum trans.) (Dordrecht: Kluwer Academic Publishers, 1998), pp. 86–87.

8 René Descartes, *Discours de la méthode* (Étienne Gilson ed.) (Paris: Vrin, 1962[1637]), p. 315.

9 Léon Brunschvicg, 'La pensée intuitive chez Descartes et chez les cartésiens' in *Écrits philosophiques*, VOL. 1 (Paris: Presses Universitaires de France, 1951[1927]), p. 58.

10 Léon Brunschvicg, *René Descartes* (Paris: Redier, 1937), p. 34.

nature as intuition, only if a common immediacy unites the *cogito* to the *Deus*, if the supreme being is, so to speak, intuitive, that intuition will not be able to escape its god and itself, it cannot but intuit itself in the divine, and, within it, divinity itself. Just as the *cogito* proceeds from the *dubito*, the 'ego (sum)' derives from the 'Deus (est)': the doubt and the god will therefore be united in the fundamental (or precisely 'concentrée' [condensed]) proposition. *Dubito, ergo Deus est*: Gilson's formula effectively sums up Descartes's, when the *cogito* cannot merely be personal, when the first person will no longer be able to be the first.

8. So much for Brunschvicg. And Guéroult? 'For Guéroult, who on this matter seemingly wanted to justify Descartes at Brunschvicg's expense, the "I think" is a thinking "I" in general, it is a general intellectual nature, a random thinking essence.'[11] As far as Alquié is concerned, he cannot be of the same opinion: 'Of course, it is true, as Guéroult observed, that the "I think therefore I am" does not necessarily mean "I am René Descartes." But, as far as I am aware, no one has been able to assert something so absurd, in the sense understood and rejected by Guéroult.' Indeed, it is obvious that after the doubt Descartes cannot affirm 'I am René Descartes': he is not sure of possessing a body, hands, a name or even a father . . . But he is certain of being an 'I'.

> Which has nothing in common with the Kantian affirmation 'I think', the famous *Ich denke*, which is a necessary link between all of my various representations. The affirmed 'I' is indeed an 'I' of mine, it is an 'I' which doubtlessly cannot be named, it is the 'I' that has experienced the 'First Meditation', the 'I' that has doubted, the 'I', if one can put it this way, that has fought again the evil genius and has resisted it, it is this subject that [. . .] was afraid of being misled and which now appears, affirms, personifies and clarifies itself.[12]

11 Alquié, *Leçons sur Descartes*, p. 153.

12 Alquié, *Leçons sur Descartes*, pp. 153–54.

Let us once again recall Paul Janet's position: when Descartes says 'cogito ergo sum' he does not add 'Cartesius' . . . I may forget my name, my age, my place of dwelling, without ceasing to be 'I', I may lose my sense of individuality but not that 'pure existence' to which the *cogito* remains tied. The thinking subject is an 'I', in Alquié's terms, because it is an 'I' that has doubted. Or rather, because in the meantime thought has never ceased to belong to the 'I': 'In the extension of the doubt I can separate from myself everything that is body, vegetative soul, etc. But that which I absolutely cannot separate from myself is thought [. . .]. Descartes [. . .] does not isolate a pure intellect [. . .] but my own thought.' Thus, his authoritative reading places stresses the *sive existo*, indicating the thinking 'I' as the true Cartesian discovery: 'It is not a pure intellect that would give being its meaning; it is a being whose attribute is thinking, *cogitatio*'.[13] It is for this reason that it can accomplish, as Foucault would say, 'a controlled exercise, mastered from the beginning to the end,' resisting and becoming more defined, beyond any doubt, as a personal thinking being. One may recall Paul Valéry:

> Never, until he came, had a philosopher so deliberately exhibited himself on the stage of his own thought, risking his own neck, daring to write 'I' for whole pages on end [. . .] applying himself to the task of describing in detail his interior debates and manoeuvres, making us participate in them, and become like himself: uncertain at first, then growing confident like him . . .[14]

And even before that, we might recall Alfred Fouillée, who in his *Descartes* had decisively rejected the possibility of impersonal thought, affirming a constant consciousness or sense of identity, independent of reflection:

---

13 Alquié, *Leçons sur Descartes*, p. 175.

14 Paul Valéry, 'A View of Descartes' in *Collected Works of Paul Valéry*, VOL. 9: *Masters and Friends* (Martin Turnell trans.) (Princeton, NJ: Princeton University Press, 1968), p. 56.

> We can sense, think, act without *reflecting* on our 'I', but we still sense it. Alfred de Musset says that 'one thinks of all of the things one loves, without knowing it'; and that is how, without knowing it, we think of ourselves. Descartes is therefore absolutely right to put his *cogito* in the first person singular and to thereby put conscience in a personal form.[15]

But a form is only ever a form, and 'the only thing that is immediate and certain [. . .] is some state of consciousness [. . .] as it is in the moment in which it occurs'. That which otherwise 'I mistake for the "subject" of thought,' Fouillée continues, with words that greatly resemble those used later by a young Jean-Paul Sartre against Husserl, 'is in reality an "object"; it is an "I" conceived and thought that I declare to be a thinking "I" and adopt as an immediate given of consciousness.'[16] And so after all of the discussions revolving around the *cogito* 'which have worried modern philosophy', a limitation imposes itself: 'I think, therefore, there is a being who thinks and who thinks himself according to the idea of the "I"—this is the only conclusion at which we can rightfully arrive'.[17] The first person of the *cogito*, as Jean Wahl will one day go on to say,

> indicates that Descartes, unlike William James when he said 'there is thinking in me', immediately notices the presence of his own person, not the person Descartes who acts and lives as Kierkegaard would define it (who for that matter would say 'I think, therefore I am not') but the person Descartes insofar as it thinks.[18]

Alquié clearly shares this position. If Wahl's focus centres on the punctuality of the *cogito* itself, the former abides by the indisputably provisory nature of the doubt and must therefore prolong it by adapting it to a

15 Alfred Fouillée, *Descartes* (Paris: Hachette, 1893), p. 100.

16 Fouillée, *Descartes*, p. 101.

17 Fouillée, *Descartes*, p. 101.

18 Jean Wahl, *Tableau de la philosophie française* (Paris: Fontaine, 1946), p. 16.

continuity that has now become biographical (from 'the "I" that has doubted' to 'the I that has lived [. . .] that has fought'). Thus, while he insists on the radical isolation of the ego (which no longer discerns anything certain around itself), he paradoxically ends up leaving it slightly less solitary, that is in the company of itself and its vicissitudes. Conceiving of the exclusive novelty of the *cogito* as an instantaneous act inseparable from doubt, he revokes the doubt right when it could subsist and undermine the very solidity of the 'I that has doubted', its certainty of being a person.

Perhaps, one might note, Guéroult had not been so naive after all. And perhaps Brunschvicg—who would go on to dedicate admirable pages in his last work to the relation between the *cogito* and Michel de Montaigne's scepticism—demonstrated his foresight, recognizing the presence of the idea of the infinite in the full evidence of being and affirming that if the hyperbolic doubt and the *cogito* are united in the intimacy of consciousness, the infinite nature of the doubt reveals the infinity of God. Or perhaps that 'pure existence' which no longer corresponds to the 'personal sense' (Paul Janet) is neither a 'there is thinking *in me*' nor an 'I' that in doubting becomes more definite and individualized; in other words, it is in no way thinkable as a 'residue of the world'.

9. 'These ideas would certainly need developing . . . ' Janet's premonition could not be satisfied by the disputes between exegetes and historians, because it was the Cartesian ideas themselves that required a new development. The existence that 'psychologists proceed from when they speak of the unity and identity of "I"' demanded nothing less than an examination capable of untying the paradox of the difference and of the inevitable identity of the transcendental and the empirical, that is, the paradox in which psychology and philosophy remained implicated, despite their presumed separation. To get closer to psychology in its purest state, what was needed was an attempt that did not limit itself to reforming it—like the one made by Franz Brentano—but which, moving from the psychology of intentionality, returned to Descartes to go beyond

Brentano, and crossing the same 'Cartesian way' abided finally by the absolute evidence of the pure 'I' and thus reached the consideration of the same operative subjectivity. That is, Janet's phrase, 'little does it matter, if he is Descartes or someone else' could not reveal its truth in the form of the subject that has doubted, has feared, has lived, who, in Alquié's words—is 'both intellect, will, imagination and sensation, in other words that belongs to the general sense of the term [. . .] consciousness.' No, at the level of the 'peu lui importe' (little does it matter), that is to say, of the *cogito*'s pure existence, the only thing that could be posited was the 'disinterested spectator', who every time reaches the undoubtable by operating the *epoché* on himself and on *his own* consciousness of the world. That 'peu lui importe' (little does it matter) could therefore only be true if uttered 'by someone who, with a certain naivety and in a certain historic situation, has been attracted, so to speak, into the *epoché*' to then find himself beyond any contingency, 'in a singular' or unplaceable 'philosophical solitude'. Thus, in Husserl's extreme vision, the ego is not a survivor of the struggle against the evil genius that 'now affirms, personifies and defines itself', but is called 'I' only due to a misunderstanding, and corresponds to the 'absolutely apodeictic' position, reachable precisely by the *epoché* itself, which with a problematic and untiring effort '*must* be actuated seriously and must *persist*'. It is not just an anonymous 'I' that is fundamental but—here, where Karl Löwith was able to recognize an idealism without an 'I'[19]—a subject that should not even be called one. Here, on the other hand, one is measuring the novelty (or lack thereof) of Azam's case: at the heart and at the same time at the limits of Husserl's research, in a solitude that recalls, and perhaps truly prolongs, maintains and resolves the frightful and strange condition suffered by Félida. It is perhaps in the mirror of the young woman's stunned and terrified gaze that the detached (*uninteressiert*) gaze of the phenomenologist will have to look at itself.

---

19 Jean Wahl, *Husserl* (Paris: Centre de Documentation Universitaire, 1958), p. 29.

10. Already in 1885, in his masterpiece *Le sommeil et les rêves*, Joseph Delboeuf had tried to correct this perspective: according to him, the Cartesian doubt is merely 'speculative', and therefore insincere, and consequently entirely unlike the doubt that the insane or the sleeping individual may suffer upon awakening; it is merely theoretical and revolves around that which, in essence, nobody doubts; entirely deprived of naivety, it presupposes the full possession of one's reason and is rather the sufficient and absolute sign of rational certainty.

Even earlier, taking a stance on the uncertain state of the *cogito* and likening it to a syllogism—as Descartes had certainly allowed, granting it 'the "allure" of reasoning' (Guérolt), but also against Descartes, who defined it first and foremost as an intellectual intuition (' . . . sed tamquam rem per se notam simplici mentis intuitu agnoscit', *Meditationes de prima philosophia, Responsio ad secundas objectiones*)—Maine de Biran had spoken of the 'fiction du doute' (fiction of doubt).[20] The Kantian echoes are obvious here: if the *Transcendental Dialectic* defined the *cogito ergo sum* as a paralogism (because existence is identified with the proposition "I think"), Biran observed that, by constructing the syllogism on the illusory basis of a unique and common *je*, Descartes confused and unduly associated the general and abstract notion of being (*je suis*) with the absolutely indubitable 'fact' (*je pense*) of consciousness or, to use his favourite expression, of the 'intimate sense'. According to Biran, Descartes's reasoning therefore is not deprived of, or lacking—as Gassendi had already remarked—its greatest premise (the implicit hypothesis 'tout ce qui pense est' [everything that thinks is]). Not only is it elliptical, or in other words an enthymeme, but—as Biran wrote, resolving in his own way the dispute between Pierre-Sylvain Régies and Pierre Danile Huet—it is nothing more than an unnecessary, fake concatenation. (Gathering together these various objections, Brunschvicg would go on

20 Marie-François-Pierre Gonthier Maine de Biran, *Commentaire sur les Méditations métaphysiques de Descartes* (1813) in *Commentaires et marginalia: XVIIe siècle*, Œuvres de Maine de Biran, VOL. 11, PART 1 (Christiane Frémont ed.) (Paris: Vrin, 1990[1813]), p. 33.

to respond that 'the *Cogito ergo sum* is not an enthymeme, because an existential proposition cannot derive from a greater one, such as: to think one must exist, to which, as expressly affirmed by article 10 of the first book of the *Principles*, no value of existence can be attributed.')[21]

At the end of the nineteenth century, however, an older criticism that was well-known to Biran and which prefigured that of Delboeuf was still in the air. For instance, Charles Jeanmaire had recently evoked it in his dissertation on *L'idée de la personnalité dans la psychologie moderne* (1882). This was the equally profound and trivial objection raised by the abbé of Lignac, who had noted that in the proposition 'I think therefore I am' the certainty of existence is anterior to its consequence since 'elle est renfermée dans le mot *je*, lequel comprend la conscience de mon existence' (it is enclosed in the word "I", which includes the consciousness of my existence). In other words, if the enthymeme is an abbreviated syllogism, the *je* is the abbreviation of the enthymeme. Hence to those who affirm with Descartes, 'I doubt, therefore I am' because it is impossible to doubt without existing, one should respond: 'That is a fallacy. If you doubt of your own existence it is only because you are lying.'[22] The response may not be very 'polie', as Lignac admitted, but it is the only one possible. Rational doubt had therefore already appeared false, or in bad faith, a whole century before Delboeuf.

What, on the other hand, is sincere is dreaming or insanity, and what is frankly dazed is the gaze of one who upon awakening from delirium struggles to recognize his loved ones. And what is undoubtable is the sole, simple 'I'. The certainty of its identity or ontological indivisibility can uniquely be guaranteed, to use a post-Heideggerian vocabulary, 'by means of the constitutive precariousness and instability of its "pure" self-utterance'.[23] A person who says 'je' affirms, in Paul Janet's terms, 'his own pure existence' with respect to which any proper name reveals itself

21 Brunschvicg, 'La pensée intuitive chez Descartes et chez les cartésiens', p. 46.

22 Abbé de Lignac, *Le témoignage du sens intime et de l'expérience* (Auxerre: Fournier, 1760), p. 41.

23 Nancy, *Ego sum*, p. 101.

to be uncertain or phenomenal. From the latter the *je* is already emancipated: it does not overshadow 'Descartes' the same way 'Descartes' does not project itself onto the *je*. In truth, 'the identity of this subject is valid only on the condition that it be identity itself, stripped completely of anything accidental or empirical (like the name René Descartes, for example) and presented in its substance as subject.'[24] And that is something which no one could doubt, no one would maintain the contrary ('such an absurd thing'). Or it might be true, on the other hand, as Husserl intuited, that even the term 'I' is consigned to equivocation. Perhaps because the fundamental sense persists tacitly behind the enunciation; it remains implicit in the *je*, it manifests itself in the *je* and it cannot but be objectified and masked by the *je*.

11. Bergson's criticism would also go on to target Hippolyte Taine and John Stuart Mill: incapable of only being psychologists, they presume to find behind the 'I'—which for them is merely a sign, the recollection of 'the primitive, and moreover very confused, intuition'—the object of a metaphysics.[25] Following Paul Janet's instructions, psychologists demand of pure existence to explain the ego without words. But the latter remains both indubitable and uncertain, identical and changing: if Descartes does not care about his own name, it is because he already knows he is R. D. and, like every other person, he knows he cannot forget doubts, fears and struggles without continuing to be an identity, either deprived of memory or with a patchy, false or secondary one. Because not only does identity not contradict the loss of personality or its metamorphoses and multiplications, but because it is precisely there, where one is alone, that the many 'I's gather in a crowd: if all scissions 'occur as the scissions of an identical egoic pole' it is because precisely the latter, which 'endures within it', is the condition of their possibility. Being multiplies itself if it is substantially identical to itself—that is, if identity has been assigned to the being.

---

24 Nancy, *Ego sum*, p. 56.

25 Bergson, *Introduction to Metaphysics*, p. 19.

Thus, psychologists' pure existence doubles and divides itself, with its many names. And under the vigilant and imposing gaze of Pierre Janet, Paul's more famous grandson, Marceline multiplies and in the meantime repeats and multiplies Félida (Jules Janet, Pierre's brother, who was the first to take her into his care, had already called her a 'Félida artificielle' [artificial Félida]), although her style is not that of alternation but of oscillation, and her most frequent states are the intermediate ones, which unfold between the rare and extreme ones of perfect wakefulness and sleep. The personalities separate and draw up opposing fronts, while between them extends the arduous panorama of life afflicted by illness, punctuated by solitary depressions and rapid rises in society.

But it is not always so. Indeed, the period of oscillation can be very brief and even imperceptible, thus forcing the two contenders into the most painful of intimacies. This is the 'complete state' that is particularly difficult to endure, and in which one day a learned American reverend, Thomas Carson Hanna, the patient of Boris Sidis and Simon P. Goodhart, found himself. On the evening of 15 April 1897, while returning home, the young, healthy and dashing Hanna suddenly fell to the ground, unconscious, without any apparent motive; rescued by his brother, he was later taken to hospital, where he remained for a few days in an unconscious state. Upon awakening, he could not remember anything about his past life and saw the world through the eyes of an infant. He had lost all of the learning he acquired since birth till the accident, and 'had to learn all over again'. After a week, Hanna was transferred to the Pathological Institute of New York State Hospital and there, under the care of Sidis and Goodhart, started to develop a double consciousness or a double personality. His old memories did not just surface in hypnotic or drugged states, but, when adequately stimulated, they also emerged in the foreground, in his upper consciousness. In this 'primary state' of his, Mr Hanna once again became in every way the learned priest that everyone had known before the incident. In the 'secondary state', however, he was the man or rather the child who had grown up from the day of the attack, still incapable of understanding the meaning of 'mine' and 'yours', of understanding sexual differences or the reason why simple gratitude and friendship can be expressed with caresses or kisses. And yet he also demonstrated an exceptional capacity for linguistic learning and an extraordinary imitative talent, thanks to which in a few hours he could become a virtuoso on an instrument he had never played before. Amnesia surrounded the two conditions and kept them strictly separate. In fact, before one personality changed over into the other, a 'hypnoletic state' of extreme sudden prostration, muscular passivity and imperturbable sleep intervened, which Sidis explains in terms of the cyclical nature of the phenomenon, as '*the reproduction of the original attack which brought about the state of double or multiple consciousness*'.[26] In the meantime, however, months passed, and the crisis underwent the strangest of evolutions: although Hanna seemed 'at times to alternate between sleep, or rather, hypnolepsy, and a state of wakefulness', his answers to the psychiatrists' questions 'indicated the presence of at times the primary and at other times the secondary state, and at times even *the presence of both simultaneously*'.[27] Until, one day, 'the two personalities, that of the first and that of the second state, appeared together to confront one another. Each of them was Hanna's "I" and yet at the same time they were different from each other [. . .] the situation became tragic and painful'.[28] While his contemporary Morton Prince was studying the conflicting lives of Miss Beauchamp,[29] Sidis observed that the different personalities fought like untiring adversaries, and yet, in that struggle, they recognized the intimate relation between them, 'if not for their *relationship of identity*. It seemed as if each said to the other, "Thou art my mortal foe, and yet thou art the bone of my bones and the flesh of my flesh"'.[30]

---

26 Boris Sidis and Simon P. Goodhart, *Multiple Personality: An Experimental Investigation into the Nature of Human Individuality* (New York: D. Appleton and Company, 1905), p. 456.

27 Sidis and Goodhart, *Multiple Personality*, p. 188.

28 Sidis and Goodhart, *Multiple Personality*, p. 193.

29 Barbara Chitussi, *Lo spettacolo di sé: Filosofia della doppia personalità* (Milan: Meltemi, 2018), pp. 181ff.

30 Sidis and Goodheart, *Multiple Personality*, p. 194.

Here, there is one too many, two opponents claiming a single property, and there can only be competition, antagonism, or at best a ceasefire, a provisional mediation. And the life that Mr Hanna is competing for against himself throws some light onto the condition of every individual subject, both bound and opposed to himself in the relation of identity. Indeed, the 'I' affirms itself as being in full possession of itself, but precisely that which mental medicine—at least since Pinel's *Traité*—calls *compos sui*, precisely the conception of the subject as self-mastery, seems to presuppose and conceal in its triumph a second or negative state, and therefore an essential doubling and an inevitable rivalry. Every victory would thus by definition be partial or provisional at best: every diurnal affirmation would be inevitably accompanied by the shadows of the latent, the subliminal, the repressed or the unconscious . . . The names had started to throng and the terminologies had begun to be defined well before Janet and Freud. But the phrase 'complete state' restores the full dominion as a struggle and even a tragic coexistence: here two is one too many and neither retreats, nothing is lost in a war without ceasefires or victories.

Here, two is one too many and, in a way that is coherent with Sidis's teaching, one recognizes in the so-called normal state the temporary affirmation of one of the contenders, that is to say a more or less prolonged but in any case provisional or apparent suspension of the conflict, an ephemeral or incomplete condition. The trick, perhaps of an enemy who operates in the meantime from the prompter's box, dictating the very mastery of their rival: the unconscious would thereby be nothing other than the condition of consciousness' possibility.

The Kantian expression 'unsocial sociability [*ungesellige Geselligkeit*]' could therefore function as a formula for individuality, or for its ontological constitution. Engaged in a perpetual struggle with its own antagonist (the strongest one at the time, among the many possible ones), the prevailing personality is constitutively crippled and aggressive, and therefore tends necessarily to associate with (*gesellig*) and at the same to time resist against those like it, whether they be external or internal, true bodies or fantastical ones, facing off against one another with mutable alliances and formations. To once again recall Kant, it thus aims at the protected situation of the *foedus Amphictyonum*: that is, at the ideal end that leaves behind it, however, the real and endless shadow of struggles and killings, which dictates Sisyphus's effort against the unbearable completeness of the first and of the last association—the former internal and usually hidden, the latter external, manifest and therefore forced to sometimes make itself secret. And like the associations, the tendency itself is both internal and external. For Robert Louis Stevenson, in the 'case' of all cases, 'man is not truly one, but truly two. I say two, because the state of my own knowledge does not pass beyond that point.' In cases equally as strange as that of Dr Jekyll and more that than that of Mr Hanna, the personalities instead of two become three or even four and at times, as we know, proliferate prodigiously to escape an unbearable completeness. The fundamental sense is a sense of hostility: pure existence divides itself into enemy factions, it multiplies and confronts itself. When identity is consigned to being, it concomitantly finds itself exposed 'to such a terrible shipwreck' (Stevenson).

. . . The constitution of the individual being refers back to fundamental being while the latter objectifies itself in personifications, names itself and is already another. If Descartes could pronounce the cogito *while ignoring his own name, it is because existence was already inscribed in identity and in enunciating itself it could not doubt itself—it already possessed the form of an ego that endures through its scissions and multiplications.*

Now, if multiplicity does not deny but rather founds and confirms permanence, this is also coherent with the possibility that opposites may manifest themselves simultaneously, as in Mr Hanna's complete state. The unity of the "I" would therefore merely be a dissimulated multitude, alternation would be a coexistence and true identity a tension between gazes fighting for the same eyes and voices that intertwine in a single breath.

The pathological condition thus shines a light on the normal one by suggesting that the dualism of soul and body sums up the struggles in which most people engage to remain alone and have to once again associate anew. It thereby teaches us, in other words, that between the individual and the social there is both more and less than an analogy, that fundamental being has always been the stage of a battle and that the subject always remains, whether in the shadows or in broad daylight, that which resists in the struggle . . . And if that were indeed the case, it would be easy to understand why the felicitous formula of dominion does not consist in the capacity to last longer than others and to erect oneself as the master personality of one's own body and of others', and therefore as stronger than all of the others, but even before that, in the provocation that makes all of the resistants themselves appear (all while arranging at the same time their coherent association), and therefore in an authentic pre-dominion, which before impressing itself on individuals animates them, or which in every moment founds the very possibility of exercising power . . .

III

The First Resistance

12. Conceiving of the human brain as a theatre in which different *pièces* are staged, Taine once again illustrated the structure of identity and its multiplications. According to the theory presented in *De l'intelligence*, every state, whether of sleep or wakefulness corresponds to a specific concatenation, a compact group of images, or, in other words, that 'which in literary and judicial language we call the moral personality'.[1] And as happens in a state of torpor or awakening, when one state merges into the next, the corresponding group of images cedes its place to the other, which can now resurface. One could thus say that a person who is awake falls at a certain point into sleep just as a sleeping one recedes and in sinking loses himself in awakening. And this losing oneself in a state of wakefulness is nothing other than the true possibility of one who is asleep: a person or association of images that takes shape and becomes a stable unit if the opposing state begins to dissipate. If in the classic, Aristotelian canon, sleep corresponds to passivity, just as wakefulness corresponds to action, if one is to believe Taine and interpret the opposition in a polar sense, one could say instead that sleep is the specific passivity of wakefulness and that the passive state that is proper to it only endures during diurnal activity.

Such an interpretation also explains the phenomenon of the 'doubling of the self', the presence of two series of parallel and independent

1 Hippolyte Taine, *On Intelligence* (Daniel N. Robinson ed.) (Washington, DC: University Publications of America, 1977), p. 97.

ideas, of two centres of action or two people who can oppose each other or appear in alternation, but on a stage that never ceases to be one and the same. Indeed, the different *moi* retain a few elements in common, they confront and ignore each other on the basis of a tacit exchange. Their affirmation will therefore not be exclusive and their alternation will not be truly absolute. If two groups of contrasting ideas or persons appear together in the same individual it is because they are not all that different after all; if one seems to disappear, it is because it can recede as the other's shadow and substrate; if it can become eclipsed it is precisely because a limit behind it nevertheless remains solid, which is that of their shared physical continuity. Thus, the dynamic of polarities and exchanges, of conquests and retreats is, in turn, based on an inert and elementary opposition: if the continuity of the physical being constitutes, in Taine's words, the permanent form or the continuity of the moral being, it is because corporeal life remains the backdrop of every retreat and alternation—the continuous and truly inactive substrate or sleep of mental activity. But this means, on the other hand, that the theatre of personal life requires the subjection or taking control of the biological organism. What defines this dominion is thus physical death, which reveals itself as both the terminus and the origin of every belonging and every possession. And that which begins from the end will never have a true beginning.

13. Émile Durkheim's conclusive sentence could also be cited in the case of Taine: 'an individualizing factor is necessary. It is the body that fulfils this function.'[2] The identity of the corporeal organization guarantees, in fact, the moral continuity and identity of the subject for the philosopher of multiplicity as well. Only if an individual fell asleep as a chrysalis and woke up as a butterfly—he argues—only if an entirely new and different organism corresponded to the new group of ideas would every continuity

2 Émile Durkheim, *The Elementary Forms of the Religious Life* (Joseph Ward Swain trans.) (London: George Allen & Unwin Ltd, 1964), p. 270.

cease and the series of images not have anything in common any more. Thus is it the impossibility of metamorphosis that explains the *dédoublement*: the human brain is a theatre because man is an infelicitous lepidopteran and is therefore incapable of making himself a pupa and freeing himself from his old body. Only a being confined to his organism, identical to itself, will one day be condemned, like Mr Hanna, to be two in one, or will be able to lose himself, becoming spiritually other all while remaining the same.

Taine reads the observations made by Maurice Krishaber, the famous pathologist who in 1873 had coined the term 'cerebral-cardiac neuropathy' in describing an illness that was still unknown but recognizable by the series of typical disturbances that afflict the sphere of sensibility only to then inevitably shift to the nervous system. It is an affliction that is often chronic, more or less acute, and capable of lasting for a number of years (without temporary returns to normality), with constant effects, and which usually ends in a complete recovery. The main symptoms affect the senses (illusions similar to those caused by drunkenness more than by delirium), and therefore locomotion (loss of balance, vertigo . . .), the circulatory system (increase in heart rate, palpitations . . .) and lastly, more or less seriously, the nervous system (irritability, insomnia, nightmares, profound sadness, a sense of anguish and oppression, cerebral over-excitement, etc.). At the heart of it, Pierre Janet would later say, this singular syndrome 'n'est constituée avec netteté que par cette unique symptôme de la dépersonnalisation' (is only clearly constituted by this unique symptom of depersonalization).[3] Nevertheless, one of the essential characteristics of cerebral-cardiac neuropathy remains the absence of any prodromes: 'the onset of the illness,' Krishaber writes, 'is sudden and extremely intense. It is well and truly a daze that afflicts the nervous system instantaneously.'[4] And, conceiving of the brain as an

3 Pierre Janet, *Les obsessions et la psychasthénie*, VOL. 1 (Paris: Félix Alcan, 1903), p. 310.

4 Maurice Krishaber, *De la névropathie cérébro-cardique* (Paris: Masson, 1873), p. 4.

organ that repeats and multiplies ideas, Taine was inevitably struck by the possibility of such a sudden disturbance. 'When the illness appears all of a sudden,' he comments, 'the effect is immense.' The intensity and the novelty—the two characteristics described by Krishaber—therefore appear to him as being mutually interdependent: the intensity of the effect derives from the novelty of the cause.

> One could not find a better analogy for the state of the patient than if a caterpillar became a butterfly and had the senses and sensations of a butterfly, all while retaining its ideas and memories as a caterpillar. Between the old state and the new, between the first 'I', that of the caterpillar, and the second, that of the butterfly, there is a profound scission, a complete break. The new sensations no longer find preceding sensations to graft onto; and the sick individual is no longer able to interpret them or use them; he no longer recognizes them—for him, they are unknown. He therefore arrives at two strange conclusions: if the first induces him to say *je ne suis pas* [I am not], the second makes him say, on the contrary, *je suis un autre* [I am another].[5]

The novelty of the condition therefore determines the peculiar acuteness of the illness because it determines it as such to begin with: the interruption of the normal moral state's continuity is pathological to the utmost extent. And the simultaneously immense and immediate effect of this destruction of one's habits becomes the loss of oneself, of the self immersed in its usual environment, or in other words the loss of a world. A patient of Krishaber's recounts: 'I looked about with terror and stupor—*the world escaped me*,' with words that would not have been out of place in the pages of Ernesto de Martino and recall the intermediate condition of Félida X, that is, the negative state of depersonalization already diagnosed by Moreau De Tours and fully admitted to the psychiatric canon by Ludovic Dugas, Théodule Ribot, Pierre Janet and

---

5 Hippolyte Taine, 'Sur les éléments et sur la formation de l'idée du moi', *Revue Philosophique de la France et de l'Étranger* 1 (1876): 289.

Fulgence Raymond, or by Eugène Bernard-Leroy who reports the 'bizarre' (that is, precise) definition—owed to 'our friend, the doctor A. B., who is quite susceptible to this impression'—of 'isolement cosmique' (cosmic isolation)[6]—which will later coherently, perhaps thanks also to Janet,[7] find its fortunes renewed in the contexts of stylistics: commenting on Théophile de Viau's *Ode*, Leo Spitzer uses precisely the expression 'kosmische Vereinsamung' to describe the way in which things appear to the gaze of the poet so loved by Gautier.[8]

For his part, Taine can explain in detail the critical shift from *dépersonnalisation* to *dédoublement*. In the 'first stage', he explains,

> the new sensations were too new; not yet sufficiently repeated to form a distinct group within memory, a coherent series, a second 'I'. Such is indeed the condition of the caterpillar [. . .] during the first 15 minutes of its metamorphosis into a butterfly; its new 'I' has not yet formed, it is barely taking shape, and the old one, which is uniquely experiencing formerly unknown sensations, is led to say: *I no longer am, I am not* . . . It will take some time for the caterpillar to get used to being a butterfly and if it keeps [. . .] all of its memories as a caterpillar, there will be a perpetual and painful conflict between the two groups of contradictory notions or impressions, between the old 'I', that of the caterpillar, and the new one of the butterfly. In the second stage, instead of saying: *I no longer am*, the patient will say: *I am another*.[9]

Whether the conflict is an open one—similar to Sidis's 'complete state'—or suspended and latent depends for Taine on corporeal sensations,

6 Eugène Bernard-Leroy, *L'illusion de fausse reconnaissance* (Paris: Alcan, 1898), pp. 173–74; Eugène Bernard-Leroy, 'Sur l'illusion dite "dépersonnalisation"', *Revue Philosophique de la France et de l'Étranger* 46 (1898): 158.

7 See Janet, *Les obsessions et a psychasthénie*, VOL. 1, CHAP. 4.

8 Leo Spitzer, *Stilstudien*, VOL. 2: *Stilsprachen* (Munich: Hueber, 1928).

9 Taine, 'Sur les éléments et sur la formation de l'idée du moi': 294.

which form the basis of signs, of images and therefore of the moral person. When these once again become the same, when the illness is defeated, he who has become another once again returns to himself, and habit is restored alongside the unity of the person. After all, a human being cannot forget itself if not by falling ill, precisely because it is incapable of a true corporeal metamorphosis. Nor will it be able to live without suffering in a state of perfect cosmic isolation, choosing a fully impersonal existence, freed from everything and always new. Caterpillar or butterfly (but at the same time still caterpillar), it can lose its habitual relation to the world and at the same time, all while suffering, it cannot but still be attached to the world. Or perhaps it is only the suffering by which the world affirms itself and imposes its own bond that forms the psychosomatic subject as such.

14. What if, however, the caterpillar and the butterfly were the same person? A century before Taine, in the heyday of sign theory, the preformist theory of Jan Swammerdam, Marcello Malpighi, Nicolaas Hartsoeker and Antonie van Leeuwenhoek had not yet been dethroned by epigenetic biology and still reflected the clear metaphysical imprint that Gottfried Wilhelm von Leibniz had impressed upon it. Thus, for Charles Bonnet, the biologist and philosopher from Geneva so admired by Lazzaro Spallanzani, the example of the metamorphosis did not disprove but rather proved the continuity and identity of the individual subject. 'If we had not followed the animal in all of its metamorphoses, if, like Swammerdam, he had not discovered the butterfly behind the caterpillar's mask, we would surely consider the personal *Identity* of the Individual with disdain.'[10] It is not in fact the visible body of the larva that transforms into a butterfly but another organic body, invisible at first, that pre-exists the fecundation and, fed by the seminal liquid, already grows and develops in the caterpillar's body like in that of

10 Charles Bonnet, *Essai analytique sur les facultés de l'âme* (Copenhagen: C. et A. Philibert, 1760), p. 464.

Lepidoptera in their adult form. This is the indestructible germ that preserves, 'très en raccourci' the elements and forms of the future organism and with which the soul is in constant relation. And so the caterpillar could never wake up all of a sudden as a butterfly and feel foreign to itself.

Now, Leibniz had affirmed, in opposition to the Cartesian school, that animals have a soul, and against the theories of doctors had distinguished the indestructibility (*indestructibilité*) and the latter's *impérissable* nature from immortality proper which is peculiar to humans ('immortalité, par laquelle on entend dans l'homme, non seulement que l'âme, mais encore que la personnalité subsiste' [immortality, whereby is understood in the case of man that not only the soul but also the personality subsists]).[11] But Bonnet wishes to venture even further, and so he separates human or reflective personality, which calls itself 'I', from its unreflective animal equivalent which is only tied to the continuity of sensations, to affirm against Leibniz himself ('he learned from the famous Swammerdam the secret of the caterpillar's metamorphosis into a butterfly, without thinking about it sufficiently . . . ') that for animals one can also speak of a conservation of the ego, that is to say 'of characters or of memory'. 'I was the first,' he affirms, overlooking the Leibnizian distinction between memory and reason, 'to show what the "I" or the Person of insects capable of metamorphosis consists of.'[12]

Bonnet was an author read and meditated on by Maine de Biran, as much as Paul-Joseph Barthez or Georges-Louis Leclerc de Buffon. And Biran is perhaps the author that we should read and meditate on the most to understand the history of the modern subject or in other words the evolution undergone at the intersection between the dualist Cartesian model and the 'vis activa' that 'conatum involvit' (Leibniz, *De primae*

11 Gottfried Wilhelm Leibniz, *Theodicy: Essays on the Goodness of God and the Freedom of Man and the Origin of Evil* (E. M. Huggard trans.) (New Haven, CT: Yale University Press, 1952), §89.

12 Charles Bonnet, *La palingénésie philosophique ou Idées sur l'état passé et sur l'état futur des êtres vivants* (Geneva: Philibert et Chirol, 1769), p. 302.

philosophiae emendatione, et de notione substantiae). Distancing himself from Étienne Bonnot de Condillac and Antoine-Louis-Claude Destutt de Tracy, Biran emancipates consciousness and volition from sensation, and together with Bonnet he re-reads Leibniz and, in opposition to both Descartes and Condillac, distinguishes man from living and sensing animals on the basis of the internal apperception of fundamental life and its related sensations. What indeed remains consistent, originating from a perspective faithful to the *Théodicée*, is that Bonnet's animal personality corresponds to the impersonal of man. And Biran is naturally familiar with the theory of degrees as expounded in the *Commentatio de anima brutorum* ('Nam praeter infimum perceptionis gradum . . . ')[13] and borrows it verbatim in the *Nouvelles considérations sur les rapports du physique et du moral de l'homme* (1820),[14] that is in the context of distinguishing between sensibility and thought, and therefore of the definition of the 'intimate sense': if thought is mere perception (proper also to animals) paired with self-consciousness or reflection, and therefore with memory, man has a permanent personal identity. Nevertheless, in deep sleep or in a state of unconsciousness, perceptions can become confused for him as well. Such states of stupor and vertiginous indistinction are similar to death, and it is only upon awakening that he regains consciousness, and begins in other words to realize that every perception is tied to another and that it belonged to him even if he did not notice it, and therefore, through consciousness or self-examination, he distinguishes perception from apperception and understands that the latter 'is not given to all souls, nor is it always the same'.[15]

13 Gottfried Wilhelm Leibniz, 'Commentatio de anima brutorum' in *Die philosophische Schriften von Gottfried Wilhelm Leibniz*, VOL. 7 (Carl Immanuel Gerhardt ed.) (Hildesheim: Georg Olms, 1996[1710]), §13.

14 Marie-François-Pierre Gonthier Maine de Biran, *Nouvelles considérations sur les rapports du physique et du moral de l'homme* (1820) in *Nouvelles considérations sur les rapports du physique et du moral Textes relatifs à la physiologie autour de 1820*, Œuvres de Maine de Biran, VOL. 9 (Benard Baertschi ed.) (Paris: Vrin, 1990[1820]).

15 Gottfried Wilhelm Leibniz, *Principes de la nature et de la grâce fondés en raison* (André Robinet ed.) (Paris: Presses Universitaires de France, 2002), §6.

It is thus from a perspective inspired in its own way more by Leibniz than by the monist perspective of the Idéologues that Biran can hatch his theoretical plot. On the one hand, overturning the major distinction made by Marie François Xavier Bichat, he associates the *vie animale* and the *vie organique*, that is to say he distinguishes them according to a difference in degree, not in nature. On the other, he borrows from Cabanis both the coincidence between the 'I' and the will and the connection between the '*impulsion énergique*' and the '*point de résistance*', which he unties however from the limits of the *économie animale*[16] to transpose it, as had already been done otherwise by Destutt de Tracy,[17] into the domain of consciousness and the will. Finding confirmation in Johann Gottlieb Fichte that the first act of the subject is voluntary and in a contemporary like Friedrich Bouterwek that individuality is a living force only knowable through the resistance that it encounters, he then transforms the *Élements d'Idéologie*'s concept of movement into the completely original concept of immanent *effort*, which he sets against the Cartesian *cogito* as an absolutely undoubtable fact. For Biran, apperception is both reflexive and at the same time immediate, because in it and only in it does the conscious 'I' (free, possessing a will) distinguish and constitute itself as such, in other words as the individual subject of an internal effort, 'non intentionné' (not intentioned), which keeps it in a 'fundamental and necessary' relation with the organism that resists against it. This is a philosophy of the act, and consciousness, to borrow the terms of the Leibnizian interpretation of Aristotle, is not a consciousness of mere action, in other words of the ephemeral form of the monad, but of a permanent force, that is, of a substantial form or entelechy. In 'ce qu'on peut appeler *force, effort, conatus*, dont l'action même doit suivre si rien ne l'empêche' (which is called *force, effort, conatus,*

16 Pierre-Jean-Georges Cabanis, *Rapports du physique et du moral de l'homme*, 2nd EDN., VOL. 1 (Paris: Crapart, Caille et Ravier, 1805[1802]), p. 340.

17 Antoine-Louis-Claude Destutt de Tracy, *Éléments d'Idéologie*, VOL. 1: *De l'Idéologie proprement dite* (Paris: Courcier, 1817[1801]), p. 153.

from which action itself must follow if nothing prevents it)[18] one can recognize what Biran would go on to call the 'force agissante et libre' (acting and free force), 'force durable' (enduring force), 'énergie durable' (enduring energy) or, according to the better-known expression, 'force hyperorganique' (hyper-organic force). As Gouhier has rightly written, Biran saved what he considered essential in Leibnizian philosophy, the definite substance as force—limiting it, however, via recourse to John Locke, to the principle of apperceptive actuality.

Biran's consciousness or 'immediate apperception' is therefore an actuality that is held back, so to speak, by the body's resistance. For this reason, it coincides with the effort; hence, to use Félix Ravaisson's beautiful formulation, the effort is not just the fundamental condition but also 'le type complet et l'abrégé de la conscience' (the archetype and essence of consciousness).[19] Such is the 'primitive fact' in which the 'I' comes to know itself as a force that impresses itself onto the organism, producing muscular movement. There is therefore no consciousness that is not consciousness of the 'I' and that is not, as Émile Bréhier summarizes, 'the intimate union of these two heterogeneous elements—immaterial force and material resistance. The ego apprehends itself as a cause in effort, inseparable from the effect which it produces.'[20]

As a singular and invariable relation between the same force and objective, between the 'hyperorganic' freedom of the will and the resistance of the corporeal mass, the *effort* is in other words, like Leibniz's substantial act, the formula for personal identity. And once again, as in Leibniz, consciousness for Biran is distinguished from the lowest level of sensation. Apperception and personality define man as such by separating him from the living being that cannot say "I". An animal, or

---

18 Leibniz, *Theodicy*, §87.

19 Félix Ravaisson, *De l'habitude* (Paris: Fayard, 1984[1838]), p. 23. English translation: *Of Habit* (Clare Carlisle and Mark Sinclair trans) (London: Continuum, 2008), p. 43.

20 Émile Bréhier, *The Nineteenth Century: Period of Systems (1800–1850)*, The History of Philosophy, VOL. 6 (Wade Baskin trans.) (Chicago, IL: University of Chicago Press, 1968), p. 53.

even a human being that has just been born, suffers and experiences pleasure all while ignoring its own vital functions; it senses without apperceiving its own sensations, *vivit et est vitae nescius ipse suae*—as Ovid's motto goes,[21] which was already dear to Montaigne and Jean-Jacques Rousseau and which Biran was able to make his own (from the 1807 *Mémoire de Berlin* to the 1820 *Nouvelles considérations*). In this Leibnizian, or indeed Aristotelian perspective, sensible life remains ineluctably at the mercy of itself and, 'enclosed in a fatal circle, it cannot but continuously spin'.[22] By contrast, being aware of his own disturbances, man does not identify with them: *je sens*, one reads already at the beginning of the *Mémoire* on the *Influence de l'habitude*, expresses the simple modification of pleasure or pain, whereas *je sens que je sens* 'designates this act by which I separate myself from my modification and recognize my "I" '. And it is precisely the reflection by which the subject thus thematizes his own difference that repeats the first separation of sentiment from sentiment. It doubles, differentiates, exposes the rift that by separating and producing the ego traverses and defines human life as such or, one could also say, illuminates and realizes the first *effort*: it is the evident resistance of the organic body that frees us every time from the *routinière* passivity or from the grip of destiny.

15. Biran's philosophy is nevertheless not a monadology, just as *effort* emancipates itself from the Cartesian paradigm of the 'acte de la *pensée*' (act of thinking). Biran admired Bonnet since his youth, calling him a 'métaphysicien observateur' (observer-metaphysician) and borrows from him the idea of the activity of the soul as a force that is applied first and foremost to the body, or in other words of free will as a 'force motrice' (moving force) acting on the fibres of the brain and on the organism in

21 Ovid, *Tristia* 1.3.12

22 Marie-François-Pierre Gonthier Maine de Biran, *Nouveaux essais d'anthropologie* in *Dernière philosophie. Existence et anthropologie. Nouveaux essais d'anthropologie. Notes sur l'idée d'existence*, Œuvres de Maine de Biran, VOL. 10, PART 2 (Bernard Baertschi ed.) (Paris: Vrin, 1989[1823–1824]), p. 152.

its entirety. And it is once again in following 'le grand observateur' (the great observer) that he distances himself from Destutt de Tracy's conception: in his view, the resistance interiorizes itself, becomes the resistance of fibres, a muscular inertia and is no longer merely directed at external objects. Volition also appears alongside this resistance of the body, so that one and the other coincide ('J'adopte entièrement sur le principe de l'effort le point de vue de [. . .] Bouterwek' [On the principle of effort, I entirely adopt Bouterwek's point of view]—letter to Joseph Marie Degérando)[23] in the ultimately evident individuality of the subject. With that characteristic gesture of his, Biran starts from the acquisitions and vocabulary of the Idéologues but—being 'both their continuator and their adversary'—overcomes the objectivism of his masters to build his own 'subjective ideology' and, going beyond Destutt de Tracy and Degérando, reach the 'point de vue vraiment idéologique [truly ideological point of view]'. Thus, when he excludes that animals may have a true personality, he may seem close to Leibniz and distant from Bonnet, but it is precisely his theory of apperception, which defines the person and therefore man as such, which is as close to Bonnet's dualism as it is far from monadology, to which it can only draw nearer from the recently-conquered subjective point of view. If Barthez's 'vital principle', for example, still harkens back to a Leibnizian order, if a 'sort d'harmonie préétablie' (sort of pre-established harmony) ties it to the organism that in its formation gradually adapts itself to it,[24] it is instead the relation between corporeal matter and consciousness that informs the lines of Biran's metaphysics. According to Gouhier's felicitous expression, Biran only encounters Leibniz once he has already discovered Biranianism, that is to say, the reign in which force and individuality are now inseparable, where force is 'force moi' (my force), power is 'puissance moi' (my power). It is when everything now proceeds from the *moi* or from

23 Quoted in Henri Gouhier, *Les conversions de Maine de Biran* (Paris: Vrin, 1948), p. 178.

24 Paul-Joseph Barthez, *Nouveau éléments de la science de l'homme*, VOL. 1 (Montpellier: Jean Martel, the Elder, 1578), p. 38.

the *effort* of the *moi* that he can borrow from Leibniz the absolute coincidence of force and being, to thus argue against Descartes and Kant (being is force, consciousness is *effort* and not just *pensée*, and in the *effort* nothing is relative, the phenomenon is indistinguishable from the noumenon), all while reserving for his ally a certain disappointment: by ignoring the first resistance, by projecting the force outside the *moi*, by ultimately 'placing the copy before the model',[25] Leibniz remained a 'métaphysicien géomètre' (metaphysician-geometrician) without ever becoming the psychologist (or the good observer) that he could have become. On the one hand, therefore, it is under the sign of Leibniz that Biran lends psychology an entirely new tone, transforming ideology into subjective ontology. On the other, faithful to the primitive and insuperable fact of resistance and of internal struggle, he repeats with Leibniz the gesture he had successfully made with Destutt de Tracy and Degérando (and in other regards with Condillac): he attempts to draw on an authentic inspiration, to reach a genuinely monadological perspective beyond the mere letter of the *Monadologia*, to find, as Gouhier also wrote, not Descartes's force-less 'I' nor Leibniz's force without an 'I' but the concrete unity of the 'I' and force. In the same way, an interpreter such as Gerhard Funke was able to cite (perhaps implicitly remembering José Ortega y Gasset) Nicola Cusano's *Deus occasionatus* on this topic, affirming that man acts by only experiencing himself as *se ipse* and that 'the doctrine of the *sens intime* [. . .] is nothing other than an occasionalism of action'.[26] What therefore remains is an 'indubitable fact': the psychosomatic individual, endowed with consciousness and a personal will, appears where a force impresses itself on its body, where a body suffers and resists.

---

25 Marie-François-Pierre Gonthier Maine de Biran, *Mémoire sur la décomposition de la pensée* in *Mémoire sur la décomposition de la pensée précédé du Mémoire sur les rapports de l'idéologie et des mathématiques*, Œuvres de Maine de Biran, VOL. 3 (François Azouvi ed.) (Paris: Vrin, 2000[1804]), p. 125; see Gouhier, *Les conversions de Maine de Biran*, p. 295.

26 Gerhard Funke, *Maine de Biran: Philosophisches und politisches Denken zwischen Ancien Régime und Bürgerkönigtum in Frankreich* (Bonn: H. Bouvier, 1947), p. 89.

16. Charles Renouvier, the pioneer of personalism and the author of the *Nouvelle Monadologie*, was very critical on this matter: 'instead of the system of monads of pre-established harmony [. . .] what is thus restored is a banal form of spiritualism'.[27] But perhaps he was not unfair to Biran when he polemically recalled the *De primae philosophiae emendatione, et de notione substantiae* (1694), that is, the famous passage on primitive force or on the cause of pre-existing movement in bodies which Gilles Deleuze would one day go on to re-read, explaining the '"lois de la courbure", la loi des plis ou des changements de direction' ('law of curvilinearity', the law of folds or changes of direction) capable of dictating from within a body the individual unity of its movement.[28] As a 'virtual action' (*agendi virtutem*) that involves effort (*conatum involvit*) and operates autonomously if it does not encounter obstacles, this force is indeed inherent in all substances and never ceases to act. From a Leibnizian point of view, no body is therefore at rest, and every created substance receives from others not the power to act but only the limitations and determinations of its virtual action or of its pre-existing effort.

Renouvier affirms—and he is not entirely wrong—that Biran has overlooked this essential idea 'which he was incapable of understanding, but which contained Leibnizianism itself'.[29] And one might therefore say that he made the *conatus* coincide with present action, separated *effort* from virtuality and the force inherent in every substance to tie it to the resistance of the body (thus also confusing external action, which for Leibniz characterizes the most perfect of creatures, with its internal counterpart). In a coherent manner, he then conceived of the absence of effort as sleep (or as habit in the sense of an excessive facility, a lack of resistance) and sleep as the absence of the 'I', thus denying the sleep of a thinking being, i.e. that which is organic or sensible and remains awake

27 Charles Renouvier, *Le personnalisme, suivi d'une Étude sur la perception externe et sur la force* (Paris: Alcan, 1903), p. 246.

28 Gilles Deleuze, *The Fold: Leibniz and the Baroque* (Tom Conley trans.) (Minneapolis: University of Minnesota Press, 1993), p. 12.

29 Renouvier, *Le personnalisme*, p. 246.

while consciousness sleeps (and when the animal, too, is asleep), any actuality or action.

In Biran's theory, there is not a trace of the force that (in its being virtual) never ceases. Instead, there is a clear break. There is one before, and there is one after. There is a time before *effort* or consciousness and it is the time of a gradual conquest, divided into three stages which, according to the 1807 *Hypothèse sur l'origine de la personnalité* (*De l'aperception immédiate*), precede the 'I', separating the simple zootype from the mixed being: the absolute domination of instinct and sympathetic reactions; the successive, gradual augmentation of muscular resistance and spontaneous action; then, the initial distinction, the first memory (a still imperfect one) of muscular sensations. And then there is an after, marked instead by the loss of the self or by the sudden 'disappearance of personal sense' that constitutes 'the true *sleep* of the thinking being', while the sensitive being—Biran explains—never falls asleep entirely if not in 'absolute death'. The before remains shrouded in uncertainty ('it is merely a hypothesis, a sign without an idea'), the after seems rather less nebulous. But if the hypothesis is thought, if the 'signe sans idée' (sign without an idea) is itself in turn an idea, then the before logically follows the after and the Biranian hierarchy of existential stages, as Étienne Souriau called it,[30] also becomes inverted and confused: the state of initial distinction, the least hypothetical one, is indeed—to use the 1807 formulation—'comparable to the imperfect reminiscence that is still attached to the vague images of a dream.'[31] Thus, it is the 'after'—consciousness, the 'I', immediate apperception, the absolutely indubitable fact—that dissipates and immerses itself in the vagueness of the 'before', in sensitive life. The sensitive is already there, it awaits consciousness,

30 Étienne Souriau, *Les différent modes d'existence* (Paris: Presses Universitaires de France, 1943), p. 28. English translation: *The Different Modes of Existence* (Erik Beranek and Tim Howles trans) (Minneapolis, MN: Univocal, 2015).

31 Marie-François-Pierre Gonthier Maine de Biran, *Of Immediate Apperception* (Mark Sinclair trans., Alessandro Aloisi and Marco Piazza intrs) (London: Bloomsbury Academic, 2020), p. 99.

and then demands to have the last word. Its finality, *its* later, is the true (historical) later and at the same time the true (logical) first, is the only *absolute* death, both of the 'I' and of the organism. That 'first' which doubles and follows the 'later' is in fact just the sleep that follows and in which every sleep immerses itself, the sleep in which the later and the before, the beginning and the end coalesce, the only sleep that can be considered complete. And the perfect absence of consciousness is not an indistinct bare life but, for the conscious being, the absence of life in which every doubleness ends. The truly indubitable fact, that is, the condition that defines the first 'fact' and every fact as such, is therefore not resistance or effort but the death of the resisting organism, and personality or 'consciousness' thereby essentially equates to the unverifiable certainty of not awakening. It is from the latter that the confused images during the first moments of awakening arise, and the vague sensitive life, the life deprived of consciousness is therefore nothing other than the shadow projected by the same myth—that is, by the fact that it will never be known as such—of organic death.

Metaphysics thus passes through psychology, the latter reaches ontology, ontology becomes personal and force becomes individual only through the (not overly explicit but efficient) introduction of the notion of death, the 'mort à la rigueur' (absolute death) (to use Leibniz's expression) which confutes the non-finite nature of metamorphoses.

What was the force or apperception, in fact? It was the consciousness of force or resistance. But what was this resistance if not first and foremost the body's inertia and therefore not just virtual movement but also the potential immobility of the body-obstacle, a mass that does not adapt harmoniously to the vital principle (Barthez) but resists in every action (even that of adaptation) because in the end it is a lifeless weight that stops force, or rather that transforms it into *effort* and by constraining it to itself makes the 'I' appear one last time? We would have good reason to ask ourselves whether 'one's body', which Biran speaks of, is not perhaps the only inevitable impediment or if in the end the immobile body, the dead body that (in a strange solution to Leibniz's *vinculum substantiale*) anchors being or force to the 'I'. We could certainly ask ourselves if it was not Biran himself who asked the same question in slightly different terms: 'What is the difference between the *living* and the *dead*, if not the force that is added to the dead individual?'[32]

It is therefore clear that corporeal death comes to define force and life as such as their specific *point de résistance*. The three stages that precede the affirmation of consciousness have their negative counterparts: that of somnambulism as the wakefulness of the animal and the sleep of the 'I', that of mere torpor or lethargy of consciousness and of the animate body during the wakefulness of its organs, and finally that of absolute sleep, in which the organs, too, shut down. In a state of *défaillance*, in magnetism, in the more or less deep drowsiness—'voilà une existence animale ou organique, absolue' (here is an absolute animal or organic existence)[33]—the I-force is still latent. In physical death—as the sleepless sleep of sleep—it becomes extinguished. It can be a momentary eclipse, an apparent separation, or a definitive one. But precisely the latter is binding, because the sleep of the thinking being (purely animal existence) is a relative modality of total sleep or of *mort absolue*. It is therefore this that truly makes individuality and resistance coincide, tying under its tyranny the virtuality of force to personal identity.

17. Biran's philosophy is not a monadology and is distinct from the latter first and foremost because of the role that it entrusts to the theory of apperception. One must remember that according to the Leibnizian idea of preformation or metamorphosis, the soul is not always rational from

32 Marie-François-Pierre Gonthier Maine de Biran, *Extrait de Reil (De organo animæ)* in *Nouvelles considérations sur les rapports du physique et du moral Textes relatifs à la physiologie autour de 1820*, Œuvres de Maine de Biran, VOL. 9 (Bernard Baertschi ed.) (Paris: Vrin, 1990[1820]), p. 171; see François Azouvi, *Maine de Biran: La science de l'homme* (Paris: Vrin, 1995), p. 411.

33 Marie-François-Pierre Gonthier Maine de Biran, *Note sur un passage très-remarquable du Teimognage du sens intime par l'abbé de Lignac* (1815) in *Commentaires et marginalia: XVIIIe siècle*, Œuvres de Maine de Biran, VOL. 11, PART 2 (Bernard Baertschi ed.) (Paris: Vrin, 1993[1815]), p. 89.

the beginning but rather becomes so in that privileged moment of conception which 'détermine ces animaux à la nature humaine' (destines these animals to human nature).[34] If beings develop or envelop, if they clothe and unclothe themselves according to changes that are usually continuous and imperceptible, conception and death are special moments, in which they either acquire or lose a lot in a single instance. Thus, all of a sudden, an animal becomes a being that is both rational, personal and immortal, whereas merely a moment earlier there was only an impersonal monad, unconscious and capable only of indistinct perceptions. But it nevertheless belonged to the history of pre-existences and metamorphoses; it was indestructible and played its own role in the theatre of pre-established harmony. Human personality and animal impersonality are in this sense united by a common dramatic vein, of which the former offers the more pronounced display: it is in fact properly 'immortal' because it stays on stage when the animal abandons its role in order to return—to use the splendid formula from *Principes de la nature et de la grâce*—to a 'théâtre plus subtil' (a more minute theatre).[35] And because all of the folds of the soul 'ne se développent pas sensiblement qu'avec le temps' (only develop perceptibly in time),[36] that which is indestructible unfolds in the immortal just as the present of the animal is pregnant with the future human.

It is therefore precisely for the pre-established harmony, which keeps the soul from changing the laws of the body and keeps the body from changing the laws of the soul, that over time the latter unites with the body, engaging with it in the least expected of relations. In Deleuze's words, 'it discovers a vertiginous animality that gets it tangled in the pleats of matter, but also an organic or cerebral humanity (the degree of development) that allows it to rise up, and that will make it ascend over all other folds.'[37] Inseparable by definition from the body, the soul can

---

34 Leibniz, *Principes de la nature et de la grâce fondés en raison*, §6.

35 Leibniz, *Principes*, §6.

36 Leibniz, *Principes*, §13.

37 Deleuze, *The Fold*, p. 11.

become personal and immortal thanks to a felicitous event in the course of infinite metamorphoses, in the universal and absolute time of the perfect agreement and harmony of monads.

According to Biran's vision, on the other hand, the appearance of the conscious being does not correspond to a sensible mutation that is temporally defined; it is instead time itself that is born with consciousness:

> There is a time, not since the modifications have appeared and begun to succeed one another, but since there is a permanent 'I' that can appreciate the series and can, in turn, produce an active modification that can be considered the first term of the series or the first ring in the chain of moments that make up the life [. . .] of consciousness.[38]

Biran's conception of time begins with apperception, coincides with the permanence of the 'I', with the affirmation of personality. If for Leibniz memory also belong to animals and lends their existence if not reason then at least continuity or a certain 'consécution' (consequentiality; the dog flees at the sight of the stick recalling the pain that it caused him), for Biran even memory is the conscious perception of continuity, and one which is 'inherent' in the initial 'distribution of force against organic resistance'.[39] The present of the effort is thus rememberable or heavy with tomorrow, and the body and soul, sensation and consciousness cannot participate in the common and infinite history of foldings and unfoldings, because if consciousness is history only the elevation of bare life to consciousness constitutes the origin of time as such. Now, time is 'born' for the conscious, unitary, personal subject, and consciousness is nothing other than self-mastery, which necessarily means that it is first and foremost possession of the body, or of the organism that resists. But the election of consciousness (of effort) to the origin and undisputed dominion over time has no counterpart in a lucid and uncontested

38 Marie-François-Pierre Gonthier Maine de Biran, *Journal*, VOL. 3: *Agendas, carnets et notes* (Henri Gouhier ed.) (Neuchâtel, Éditions la Baconnière, 1957), p. 219.

39 Maine de Biran, *Mémoire sur la décomposition de la pensée*, p. 158.

affirmation over the sensible sphere or a free and definitive primacy of the will over the corporeal mass. A total, complete domination would, by definition, be without time and without history, and its beginning would coincide with the end, yielding a stasis without a future. The 'I' persists, however, when its emanation remains alive, if the resistances of the body and the conditioning of the climate succeed each other, or if in the most quotidian of gestures gradual yieldings of the will insinuate themselves. And its comedy is not played out on the universal stage of metamorphoses but in the small theatre of individuality, which is small and already overcrowded: here, in fact, *two* forces 'without transforming one into the other act together; each remaining within its own domain, they conspire, oppose each other, fight, and every once in a while, triumph. Who of us is not, at every moment, an actor and witness of this internal scene?'[40] A fact—the fundamental fact, the primitive antithesis between action and resistance—is nothing if it is not known, Biran observes. The affirmation is echoed by a comment of Maurice Merleau-Ponty's: there is no fact without a witness, if it refers to someone.[41] One is therefore dealing with a non-neutral, partisan witness, precisely because it is his force or knowledge that, without being able to overcome it, has at least reduced its antagonist to mere resistance. It is here that the story of the 'irreducible'[42] duality, or of the being that is double precisely when it is one and says 'I', is inaugurated and plays out. If man is indeed the animal that, when it ceases to grope among opaque presentiments, liberates itself from destiny and founds time, it is also true that it is precisely to him that the body shows itself in illness as it is, as a resisting mass. It is under the 'rayon direct de la lumière de conscience' (direct ray of the light of consciousness)—according to the formulation in *Note sur l'idée*

40 Maine de Biran, *Mémoire sur la décomposition de la pensée*, p. 383.

41 Maurice Merleau-Ponty, *The Incarnate Subject: Malebranche, Biran and Bergson on the Union of Body and Soul* (Jacques Taminiaux pref., Paul B. Milan trans., Andre G. Bjelland Jr. and Patrick Burke eds) (Amherst, NY: Humanity Books, 2001), p. 69.

42 Merleau-Ponty, *Incarnate Subject*, p. 69.

d'existence, perhaps the last of Biran's works[43]—that a 'simple life' remains obstinate. There is no sensibility without an 'I' or an 'I' without sensibility,[44] and if the origin and form of time coincide with personality, it is only with the will and freedom of the person that the history of the bond that ties a being to its body begins. When it overcomes the lowest step of indistinction, when its 'shadow' appears, existence become a double affair, one that is tied to itself, and it illuminates itself as a consciousness in a time that both flows and remains blocked.

Biran borrows Herman Boerhaave's formulation: *homo simplex in vitalitate et duplex in humanitate*. And while he develops his writings around this theoretical linchpin, he lives in the grip of 'the alternation of domination by the body and self-mastery'.[45] But even the formula is circular and revolves around itself: man is double being *simplex* (in his being organic) and at the same time *duplex* (in his being conscious, that is, human), and consciousness is therefore always enveloped in duplicity from the very beginning. Man is double, that is, being on the one hand a simple monad, a sensitive being that—in its animality—becomes all of his affections or identifies with them ('and therefore immediately suffers the good or ill of *being*')[46]—and on the other the intelligence and consciousness of his own duality, that is to say an impotent witness of the internal scene. The witnessed simplicity is, however, a duplicity that is in turn manifest to consciousness in such a way that the double individual is at least triple, if the infinite regression—an ancient problem and a modern threat of a thinking of the self that is no longer divine—were not stopped in the presentness of the *effort* when the two do not become three, with one remaining the witness and strict guardian of the other: one because it sees and the other precisely because it cannot see. The conscious force thus ties itself to brute resistance, freedom affirms itself

43 Maine de Biran, *Nouveaux essais d'anthropologie*, p. 225.

44 Merleau-Ponty, *Incarnate Subject*, p. 71.

45 Bréhier, *Nineteenth Century*, p. 52.

46 Maine de Biran, *Mémoire sur la décomposition de la pensée*, p. 385.

as long as there is constraint and destiny, there is personality as long as there is the comparison with organic animality: the individuality of the subject owes its duration precisely to duplicity. And for the consciousness that endures in the effort, actuality is both a fortress and a prison. And yet there would not be any actuality if there were not an elementary disparity and duality, if the two extremes were not maintained at their due distance. The separation must be as defined as possible, the duality simple and clear. Thus, the reduction of the animal to the organic and of the organism to resistance and inertia, the definition of sleep as 'absolue' animality and the furtive, ambiguous but all the less ignorable apparition of death (the true sleep of sleep) are strictly functional for the affirmation of consciousness, for the constitution of the indubitable fact as such.

If, for Leibniz, one life transformed and developed into another in the process of conception, in the time of the Biranian *moi* the reduction of animal existence to a resisting force coincides with the elevation of consciousness to a hyper-organic level. One emerges only from the degradation of the other, so that, returning once again to Deleuze, it is precisely the animality that dazes and envelops in the folds of organic matter that retains its witness: the 'sensibilité sans moi' (sensibility without the I) does not define an indestructible life but remains tied to the personal consciousness that it guards in the meantime. Leibniz's force is impeded by, or rather anchored to the 'I', and the permanence of a bond can thus supplant the process of metamorphoses, while elementary dualism becomes a primitive antithesis that opens and maintains a gap between the obscurity of simple life and the luminosity of consciousness. Suspended between now-separated essences that are incapable of merging, this is the interval of the pure and insuperable relation, in which self-mastery and the dominion of the body alternate. It is not the complex and harmonious relation that the genius of monadology could discover between the body and the soul (soldering them, however, with the *vinculum* that escapes every relation), and which in uniting the body to the soul mutates into new folds and unfoldings, but the simple one between low and high, between organic obscurity and the light of the hyper-organic, and without which the second term too would be unthinkable, and therefore a relation for the sake of a relation, which maintains itself, almost in tension and yet already blocked or incapable of real development. Once again, if the formula *homo duplex in humanitate* is in and of itself exposed to a *regressio*, if consciousness multiplies through *dédoublements*, it is precisely this possibility that plays in favour of individuality when it remains close to its opposite, bound to the efficient resistance of the organism that lives or dies. *Compos sui* is a restrained depersonalization, a latent proliferation of the *alter* currently and tiresomely inhibited by reference to the body, or in other words, a force that becomes an *effort* because it is ordained or held back by organic influence, by passivity and physical suffering. Thus, all of the possible multiplications repeat and amplify the first *doublement*, they go back and cling into the insuperable tension of the *duplex* and the *simplex*.

If man is double, then the essence of duplicity, in which alone consciousness or the essence of humanity is affirmed, is nothing but the pure, present relation: 'the very basis of our being, from which we cannot separate ourselves, is a mixture or a relation.'[47] Thus, 'the principle of effort, which is constitutive of the state of wakefulness, although it cannot be conceived as other than hyper-organic or superior to the organs in its free determination, remains [. . .] up to a certain point tied to the laws and the dispositions of the organs that it acts upon'[48] and true personality, the identity of the conscious being, which can only be distinguished thanks to the power of the temperament that assails it,[49] emerges, in its daytime profile, from an obscure existence that continues to exist alongside only to irrupt into hallucination, into maniacal delirium and

47 Maine de Biran, *Note sur un passage très-remarquable du Teimognage du sens intime par l'abbé de Lignac*, p. 310.

48 Marie-François-Pierre Gonthier Maine de Biran, *Nouvelles considérations sur le sommeil, les songes et le somnambulisme* in *Discours à la société médicale de Bergerac*, Œuvres de Maine de Biran, VOL. 5 (François Azouvi ed.) (Paris: Vrin, 1984[1809]), p. 89.

49 Maine de Biran, *Mémoire sur la décomposition de la pensée*, p. 92.

into madness, and lords it over the life of the imbecile, who suffers these afflictions while his 'moi sommeille' (I slumbers), or in that of the idiot, who by contrast lives and feels, and even experiences 'the entire cycle of sensitive existence' beyond which, however, 'there is nothing' for him[50] and finally manifests itself, as the sovereign power, in convulsive movements, in somnambulism or in habitual automatism, when an acquired facility almost eliminates effort, undermining the fundamental relation between *sujet* and *terme*, between driving force and organism. The first distinction, by which the 'I' affirms itself, inaugurates time and gives liberty. And it also yields, in the same restrained leap, the relation with *simplicité native* or physiological affectivity. The consciousness of the body is the apparition of time as the continuous attestation of the bond that ties one to the other.

Once again: Biran can free substance from the overly-objective, material view that Descartes and Nicolas Malebranche had of it, and conceive of it in a purely intellectual or *sur-animal* sense only by drawing it closer to the antithetic pole of corporeal mass, tying activity to passivity in effort, the agent to the act, the (voluntary) cause to the domination of its own (organic) effect, the judgement to the passive imagination. Spiritual liberty recalls the gravity of the organism, the will actuates itself only to lose itself in sleep, in distraction, or in *routine*.

. . . *For there to be conflict, 'il faut un facteur d'individuation. C'est le corps que joue ce rôle' (there must be a factor of individuation. It is the body that plays this role). It was Maine de Brian who re-thought Cartesian dualism and understood that the bond between consciousness and the body could be guaranteed by the continuous transformation of vital* dynamis *into* effort. *Biran goes back to Leibniz: if in the theatre of monads everything is force* (vis viva *or* vis mortua, *primary or derived force*), *if universal* dynamis *does not require an external stimulus because it has in*

50 Maine de Biran, *Mémoire sur la décomposition de la pensée*, p. 95.

itself the entelechy and, as the middle term between the faculty of action and the act, implies the conatus, *Biran's force impresses itself however onto its resistance and only defines itself through it, because it is in and of itself distinct and double, it is force only in light of consciousness and therefore, in 'fact', force and light together, the force of the spirit applied to the resistance of the body. The theories of pre-established harmony and metamorphosis also had to be transformed in a coherent manner: the internal tension had to tie consciousness to the organism and a struggle for domination had to ensue between the two. The position of the current ego became that of both a witness and simultaneously a protagonist of the same conflict, it was the situation of self-consciousness, busy combatting the body's resistance (since immanent effort is nothing other than a new mode of apperception: a manifestation and at the same time a scission or duplication of force). It is in fact in the domain of the insuperable antithesis that duplicity and individuality cannot contradict each other; instead, they remain strictly coherent over the course of a duration defined by the resistance of the organism or by the death that suffocates it. Hence the rhetorical question: 'Qu'est ce qu'une organe vivant en lui-même sans une force qui s'y applique?' (What is a living organ in and of itself without a force applied to it?). A question that takes up and transforms Cabanis's proposition: there can be no energetic impulse without a point of resistance. Now, in reality, it is the force that by exerting itself divides and doubles itself in its corporeal resistance, it is the living being that doubles and defines itself by superimposing itself perfectly on itself, the presses onto itself, applies or resists itself. But to split oneself and appear as such this organic force must, in turn, project the negative double of the lifeless body. Here, conflict reigns, and conflict dethrones harmony, where a new configuration of* dynamis, *no longer immortal because no longer virtual, determines the double structure of the subject; thus, once again, 'the experience of individuality in modern culture is bound up with that of death.'*[51]

51 Michel Foucault, *The Birth of the Clinic: An Archaeology of Medical Perception* (A. M. Sheridan Smith trans.) (New York: Random House, 1973), p. 197.

IV

The Time of Force

18. Maine de Biran's true discovery was that the distinction of personal identity, of the subject endowed with consciousness, coincides with doubleness itself. The form of time unfolds in memory and dates back to the sense of identity, that is, to 'immediate internal apperception', to the consciousness of a force 'qui est *moi*' (that is *me*) and of a 'substance passive avec laquelle le *moi* ne fasse qu'un' (passive substance with which the I is one). But the history of the conscious person, of that which is called *compos sui*, is for that same reason a history full of lacunae, a history of the exhausted consciousness. It is not by chance that Biran specifically chose the term *effort* to indicate the 'fact' that is constant and equal to itself—a term that, as Bréhier underscored, would seem to suggest rather an exceptional, discontinuous state, a relatively brief interruption of the flow of consciousness.[1] If the *effort* is not a mere suspension it is because that very same animal or vital sensitivity is 'a completely primitive, *sui generis* fact'.[2] Surrounded since forever by 'obscure sensations' and without time, conditioned by the tendencies of character—which Biran, following Bichat, calls 'the physiognomy of temperament'—the lucidity of the will must always strive and struggle to be itself and to act. In the meantime, the mirror of the universe in the theatre of pre-established harmony turns opaque and blind in a single point: a ray of the 'lumière

1 Bréhier, *Nineteenth Century*, p. 55.

2 Maine de Biran, *Nouveaux essais d'anthropologie*, p. 66; see Bréhier, *Nineteenth Century*, p. 58.

de conscience' (light of consciousness) remains immersed in the shadows of organic life because the latter, which captures it, 'does not show its reflection to us'.[3]

Vital simplicity is obscure and obscure to itself: *Vivit et est vitae nescius ipse suae*. But consciousness lacks serenity and its light is an elegiac one. Biran, as we have said, repeatedly cites Ovid's verse from the *Tristia* (1.3.12)—probably taking it from *Emile*[4]—or better yet the *tristissima noctis imago* of the poet banished from Rome. It is the evening of the last farewell: the *supremus tempus* of undefinable length, close to the end and suspended in a stunned torpor, in which Ovid, as if struck by Jove's lightning, lives without knowing that he is alive. Here, in the Latin *stupor*, one finds reflected the *étourdissement* or the *stupeur* of the simple monad that Cartesians, according to Leibniz, confused with death itself, and one can perceive, in all of its Biranian nuance, the state of somnambulism as unconscious life deprived of will. All the same, this stupor can be recognized in consciousness, and consciousness is only consciousness of stupor. *Vivit et est vitae nescius ipse suae* . . . But Ovid immediately adds: *Ut tamen hanc animi nubem dolor ipse removit*. We have seen that Biran distinguishes between 'the sentient being that suffers or rejoices without reflecting on itself, without being able to say "I"', from the state of 'apperception, in which the subject, as if shaken in his organization, senses or perceives himself, is conscious of a modification and therefore does not identify with it.' *Ut tamen hanc animi nubem dolor ipse removit, / et* [. . .] *sensus convaluere mei* . . . the cloud (the obscurity or daze) is removed when suffering (caused by the lightning bolt) supplants itself as the perception of the pained 'I'. Suffering as an evident modification, that is the resistance of the suffering body, foreshadows vigilance, and the return to one's senses is sense awoken into consciousness in the double being.

---

3 Maine de Biran, *Mémoire sur la décomposition de la pensée*, p. 92.

4 Anne Devarieux, 'L'exil des affections pures: À propos d'une formule d'Ovide et de sa reprise biranienne', *Revue philosophique de Louvain* 103(1–2) (2005): 139–40.

As distinct from sensation as it is inseparable from it, consciousness is therefore a suffering of suffering, or in other words, so to speak, the sensation of the pained 'I' itself. We already recalled the famous note of the *mémoire* on the *Influence de l'habitude*: the expression *je sens* expresses the simple modification of pleasure or pain, whereas *je sens que je sens* designates the act 'by which I separate myself from my modification, and recognize my "I" '. In this original revisitation of Leibniz's theory of apperception, or in this distorted version of the 'thought in thought', consciousness is *awoken to itself* in suffering and precisely insofar as it is a consciousness of sensation it cannot be other than a consciousness of consciousness (*je reconnais mon moi*), a clarity that is in turn evident in the distinction: 'I declare that I have the sensation of a composite or double existence whose two terms are truly inseparable.'[5] The *sensus convaluere mei* operates here as the canon of the 'sense of a double existence' in which consciousness is both the intellectual perception of the doubleness and the sensitive evidence of suffering. The terms are therefore truly inseparable: there can be no sensitive life, which only suffers or experiences pleasure, if not as the life and passion of consciousness, or as living the consciousness of pain. There is no active consciousness that is not in turn pure passion (just as there is no will that is not simultaneously evidence of habitual and involuntary action) and there can only be an 'I' or personality when one distinguishes an impersonal life that is ignorant of itself.

But this doubleness must first and foremost be recognized in its fundamental ambivalence: as a self-possession (*compos sui*) that is not just action but also, in and of itself, passivity. If Descartes, as Bréhier observes, thought he had uncovered a reflection of the self on itself that was entirely independent from the action of a cause on the body, thus isolating the thinking substance, as a thing, from *res extensa*, Biran revealed that every consciousness is an effort to overcome resistance or,

5 Marie-François-Pierre Gonthier Maine de Biran, *Notes sur le Premier Problème de la Philosophie* in *Commentaires et marginalia: XIXe siècle*, Œuvres de Maine de Biran, VOL. 11, PART 3 (Joël Ganault ed.) (Paris: Vrin, 1990[1813–1815]), p. 206.

one might gloss, that reflection, as self-possession, requires a term to refer to, that the interrupting act of freedom remains integral to the extension of passive life. But consciousness or *compos sui* must also appear as the limpid, manifest affirmation of activity over passivity, rejecting and dissimulating the latter in the body's stunned condition: the liberated luminosity of the will thus projects its characteristic, crepuscular shadow.

Everything therefore depends on the dominion of action, on the predominant nature of consciousness: the first cause is the actuality of the cause or the force as active principle and affirmation; and the first effect is precisely the transposition of passivity from consciousness to its correlate—a concealment that translates (betrays) itself into the obscurity of animal life. If in fact the latter resists as a '*sui generis* fact' belonging to the same level as actual force, it is because its passivity is that of consciousness itself, which has concealed itself in organic forms and lives within them under a false name.

For this reason, once again, the figure of the *homo duplex*, composed of will and distraction, personality and impersonal life, is in itself both simple and double or fundamentally ambiguous: a sediment and mask of consciousness, its dominion, and at the same time already uncertain. Or a punctual continuity of the *cogito*, which however always requires an additional effort, since the relation with animal life is a matter of the relation of force to itself; or else a search for equilibrium that will have no end, since it is itself double and unbalanced. It is true, as one reads in the *Conversation avec MM. Degérando et Ampère* (1813), that

> ever since I say *I* [. . .] I recognize my identical, durable, permanent being, and am in my own eyes much more than a phenomenon and hence the *object* or immediate end of the constitutive force of the 'I' is more than a phenomenon: it has the permanent existence and the fixity of an *object* and of a *thing*.[6]

6 Marie-François-Pierre Gonthier Maine de Biran, *Conversation avec MM. Degérando et Ampère* in *Rapports des sciences naturelles avec la psychologie et autres écrits sur la*

All the same, this I-thing obviously only remains such by identifying itself with the subject of an *effort* that in itself will never be reified or concluded. It therefore requires *encore un effort*, one capable of believing in its own product. It is thus true that from the *Rapports des sciences naturelles avec la psychologie* (1813–15) onwards, by becoming ontological psychology itself 'provides itself with *croyance*'[7] in a substance, in a reality in itself that (against Kant) becomes accessible through effort and subsists beyond it, too, when there is no longer any consciousness of the 'I'. But this is clearly a deferral and it is precisely the postponed contradiction that is already accepted. If something first and foremost remains it is thus an incoherence, or better, as Gouhier has underscored, a 'discontinuité du moi phénoménal à l'âme nouménal, de la connaissance à la croyance' (discontinuity between the phenomenal I and the noumenal soul, between knowledge and belief).[8] For Biran, the continuity is discontinuous and demands an effort in which it simultaneously loses and finds itself, and remains unreachable, because it is precisely its discontinuity that cannot be other than constant. Thus, duplicity is in turn and in itself ambiguous, and the time of consciousness is that of an equally necessary and impossible search essentially dictated by bare existence without time, which is destined to end and, thus ceasing, to put an end to time or to the *prise de conscience*. 'Chacun devrait avoir un art de vivre' (Everyone should have an art of living), Biran writes echoing once again Bichat. And he adds: 'mais on ne le connaît guère que quand il *est temps* de *mourir*' (but we only come to know it when *it is time to die*). This art is therefore an inopportune, always incongruous habit, one that is late ever since the beginning if death, to use the famous formulation, is '*certain and as such indeterminate*' and life or the history of consciousness can always flow back into the whirlpool of its absence. For Descartes,

---

psychologie, Œuvres de Maine de Biran, VOL. 8 (Bernard Baertschi ed.) (Paris: Vrin, 1986[1813]), p. 222.

7 Azouvi, *Maine de Biran*, p. 317.

8 Henri Gouhier, 'Maine de Biran et Bergson' in *Études sur l'histoire des idées en France depuis le XVIIe siècle* (Paris: Vrin, 1980[1948]), pp. 107–8.

time coincided with the actuality of thought while self-conservation was in act only in the divine being (*causa sui*) and the future of consciousness, the guarantee of its duration, depended on the active *vis* of God: the atomistic instant of the *cogito* therefore corresponded to the divine action of *conservatio*. For Biran, as we have seen, there is instead time 'dès qu'il y a eu un moi permanent': but this is a *supremus tempus*, both held back in the effort and conceded and threatened by a master more powerful than any effort.' 'Supprimez la résistance, vous supprimez la conscience' (get rid of resistance and you get rid of consciousness), Bréhier wrote on the subject and the phrase is perfectly calibrated because it is both true and rhetorical at the same time: the resistance remains in fact insuppressible, because that which resists against consciousness is the dying body, and its death coincides with the only, impossible possession of consciousness.

19. We ought to learn something from Biran's teaching. The *dédoublement* does not derive from a defect of the 'I', of its stable possession. Every empirical or pathological doubleness originates in the fundamental duality of the being that is a conscious master of itself, it comes from the necessary repetition and dissemination of the latter in multiple forms. Free will and habit or distraction, the afflictions of the body that disturb the mind, the philosopher's life in a countryside house and the inappropriate one as a highly-placed state official ('C'est presque un autre moi' [It is almost another I], 'Je suis dans la société comme un somnambule' [I am in society like a somnambulist]), in other words Grateloup and Paris—two places or 'two internal worlds' and their unsolvable alternation. 'J'y ai gagné, sous le rapport matériel [. . .] J'ai perdu le *conscium* et le *compos sui*' (I have gained materially from it [. . .] I lost my *conscium* and my *compos sui*)[9]—Biran wrote well before Bergson (in the *Essai sur les données immédiates de la conscience*) would come to speak

9 Marie-François-Pierre Gonthier Maine de Biran, *Journal*, VOL. 1: *Février 1814–31 décembre 1816* (Henri Gouhier ed.) (Neuchâtel: Éditions la Baconnière, 1954), p. 37.

of our two 'I's, of which one is the external projection, the spatial and social representation of the other; and in such a way he shed light on the situation and the emotional tonality of consciousness: the sad Ovidian night, in the imperious dominion of the *imago*. If indeed consciousness is always already related to itself, the immediacy is lost in the image. 'The I does not objectivize itself at all in an image [. . .] But when we wish to go back to the origins of this sensed effort [. . .] we only really grasp the image.'[10]

What is thus actualized is a continuous inversion of the flow of time, or better yet, a production of the origin by virtue of which the substantial act precedes any particular action, because every single one is pre-existed by the resisting mass of the organism which consciousness itself reveals: 'In every one of my decisions,' Biran writes in a passage admired by Ravaisson,

> I recognize myself as the cause that is anterior to its effect and that will survive it; I see myself beyond, outside of the movement that I produce, as if I were independent of time; and this is because, properly speaking, I am not becoming, but really and absolutely am.

I am always already present to myself, or in other words always already in a struggle with my body; I am real and absolute and not immortal in Leibniz's sense, because I cannot become it. Held back in an already saturated time that is conscious of me and subject to me, I exist in the supreme moment, in the hour of continuous effort, which does not pass because it is the last one. And it is always the last one because it continuously overtakes the ever-undefinitive image of itself.

The statute of the Ovidian image, the statute of memory, corresponds in that sense to the continuous register of Biran's writing, from his philosophical words to the *Journal*. In fact, one could gloss that he remains essentially diaristic even in his main philosophical definitions. Indeed,

10 Maine de Biran, *Mémoire sur la décomposition de la pensée*, p. 425; see Merleau-Ponty, *Incarnate Subject*, p. 87.

the stability of every formula appears continuously exposed to the test of the diary and every time everything turns out to be a pure relation, every affirmation rings out '*double* et non plus *simple*'. Thus, a page of the *Nouvelles considérations sur le sommeil, les songes et le somnambulisme* (1809) responds to Buffon's monologue of the first man, who fears he has left something of himself in his sleep: 'May this man on the verge of being born be reassured: one does not lose anything in sleep, and one re-finds one's entire existence, one's "I" entirely whole as soon as one begins to act and will.'[11] And these words are punctually echoed by another passage in the *Journal*, written ten years later: 'I am no longer "I", I search for myself upon awakening from a sleep that has restored me from the agitations of the night before and I cannot find myself.'[12] There will be no definitive verdict: the first loses itself in the second while the latter finds its answer in the former.

Hence the constant return to the same themes, the perennial dissatisfaction with which the philosopher Biran revisits and rewrites his pages. They all remain incomplete because, like every line of every diary, they are suspended on the edge of death. Immediacy is thus granted as an *imago*, while the *imago* never attains immediacy. What is, in fact, the 'I'? 'Le *moi* n'est que . . . ' (The I is merely . . .) Biran responds to the obvious or latent question with an endless work. But this diaristic work, imagistic and veiled by sadness, finds itself in turn inexorably exposed to the question, and contains the no less ineluctable confession of defeat in the face of its direct enunciation:

> On 25 November [1817] I spent the evening at *abbé* Morellet's. A psychological conversation. My old friend abruptly asked: *what is the I*? I was unable to respond. One has to adopt the

11 Maine de Biran, *Nouvelles considérations sur le sommeil, les songes et le somnambulisme*, p. 83.

12 Marie-François-Pierre Gonthier Maine de Biran, *Journal*, VOL. 2: *1er janvier 1817–17 mai 1824* (Henri Gouhier ed.) (Neuchâtel: Éditions la Baconnière, 1955), p. 248.

> point of view from within consciousness [. . .] then [. . .] one can perceive this "I" and one no longer asks *what it is.*[13]

This is the 'moving testimony of the impotence of language'[14] and—as such—of its insuperability, it is the paradoxical expression which retains the memory of the insurmountable question and of the nevertheless impossible answer. Man is subject to an eternal and vain psychological conversation, one that is about language and the *imago*, and to truly adhere to himself, to place himself in other words, once and for all, within consciousness, he would have to paradoxically die and survive himself. Morellet's explicit question is in fact already the implicit question inscribed in every sign and which resounds in every word. The *what is it*? arises where the light of consciousness originates, in the visual that is mine and already not mine: 'je me vois en deçà' (I see myself below), 'nous n'embrassons [. . .] que l'image' (we embrace nothing but the image).

Certainly, the periods of Biran's thought are clearly distinguishable: the phase oriented towards pure psychology differs from the later religious one, dominated by 'Augustinian-Cartesian-oratorical' tones and motifs.[15] But in the diary-work, the objectivized 'I' and the act of writing nevertheless maintain an unresolved relationship, the step 'hors du moi' that is necessary to describe states of consciousness remains paradoxically tied to the *effort* by which it is accomplished, the *sens intime* of tension and concentration with which one obtain the 'series of fragments, notes, more or less schematic and symbolic representations' cannot be separated from the series itself: ontology therefore cohabits with psychology, psychology cohabits with metaphysics, unity with plurality, spiritualism with empirical observation, just as self-possession cohabits with alienation and consciousness with ecstasy. It is in the impossibility of getting to the bottom of the effort that the possibility of the later mystical state

13 Maine de Biran, *Journal*, VOL. 2, p. 95.

14 Wahl, *Tableau de la philosophie française*, p. 74.

15 Funke, *Maine de Biran*, p. 134.

originates, and it is once again the voice of the body that, by giving way, makes itself heard in the divine voice: 'Being weak,' one reads once again in the *Journal*, 'I am better able to feel the influence of a spirit that is not my own.' The doctrine of the *sens intime* announces the mystical exit from oneself and 'the soul is not separate from either its body, its counterparts, its own effort, or from God.'[16] Nothing escapes, no distinction can avoid the law of impossible cohabitation.

20. One could also ask another question: why is consciousness self-consciousness and why by objectifying itself in the reflection of the I does it dissimulate its own passivity in its dominion over the body? What is this dominion founded on and what does its unresolved economy originate from? Let us remember Max Stirner's famous words on the *spiritual* man:

> His life [. . .] is—*thinking*; the rest does not bother him; let him busy himself with the spiritual in any way that he can and chooses—in devotion, in contemplation, or in philosophic cognition—his doing is always thinking; and therefore Descartes, to whom this had at last become quite clear, could lay down the proposition: 'I think, that is—I am.' This means, my thinking is my being or my life; only when I live spiritually do I live; only as spirit am I really, or—I am spirit through and through and nothing but spirit. Unlucky Peter Schlemihl, who has lost his shadow, is the portrait of this man become a spirit; for the spirit's body is shadowless.—Over against this, how different among the ancients![17]

The *a priori* is historical, and self-intuition can contain a syllogism and the syllogism can be developed by the spiritual subject or seem uncertain and reduce itself to an enthymeme. Such a devaluation, being so to speak

16 Wahl, *Tableau de la philosophie*, p. 82.

17 Max Stirner, *The Ego and Its Own* (David Leopold trans.) (Cambridge: Cambridge University Press, 1995), p. 24.

internal, cannot be overlooked: thought therefore prepares itself for a new undertaking, makes an effort, both necessary and paradoxical, that is aimed at restoring to the spirit its shadow. And if at least Peter Schlemihl travelled through the word with fable-like levity, the now-uncertain spiritual subject, lacking seven-league boots, will have to endure and overcome his entire bodyweight. The unity of the soul and body, which defined the theological unity of the person, will now be the result of the former's action on the second: the *moi* will consist exclusively in the *effort*. The substantial act will become instead a substantial effort that absorbs all thought, that identifies with thought endowing it with now-physical connotations (it is Renouvier who will contest Biran's conception of the will as a transitive force, 'physically realized to transmit movement to the organs').[18] And because here 'all of thought' means 'all of life', marked by the senses and by afflictions, defined by the double caesura of birth and death, Maine de Biran will go on to write his diary-work.

But the historical *a priori* of spirituality recalls, in showing itself, a bigger story, in which Stirner is also involved. It is the lengthy modern affair of property, which we can summarize here at least partially in a brief conceptual stemma.

It was Georges Canguilhem who showed the extent to which the *Je pense donc je suis* remains inseparable from the Cartesian theory of the animal-machine: the definition of the subject as a thinking being or of the soul as a judging being is the correlate of the impossibility of attributing a soul to beings who do not seem to possess the faculty of judgement, inventive capacity, or authentic language. The indubitability of the *cogito* thus closely corresponds to the man/animal partition (and therefore the man/animal one in man), since the *cogito* is a natural light, *intuitus mentis* ('auquel seul je tiens qu'on se doit fier' [in which alone I believe we must trust]) and not an instinct, a natural impulse to protect the body or directed at corporeal enjoyment, etc. ('lequel ne doit pas toujours être suivi' [which must not always be followed]). The apodeictic nature of the *cogito* establishes in other words a separation and establishes an

18 Renouvier, *Le personnalisme*, p. 248.

equally indubitable order, abandoning the body and the animal to the dominion of the mind and of man. Thus, as Canguilhem once again writes, recalling the animate *organon* of the *Politics*—'Descartes does to the animal what Aristotle did to the slave: he devalorizes it in order to justify its use by man as an instrument'.[19] Now, the Aristotelian paradigm whereby the slave is reduced to an instrument, is notoriously the relation between the soul and the body. Indeed, the former exercises a despotic command over the latter, just as, within the soul, the intellect exercises a truly basilic and political authority over the appetites. The constitution of this dominating power, of property—of the economical *arché*, in other words—as a natural, non-violent power, thus occurs in the *Politics* via an exemplary transfer, at the heart of animality itself, of the relation between the spiritual and the corporeal: that is, in the name of the soul's authority over the obedient body. To affirm, as Canguilhem does, that 'Descartes does to the animal what Aristotle did to the slave' means implicitly maintaining that (through the man/animal distinction) he did with the soul and the body that which Aristotle (through his own hierarchical soul/body distinction) had done precisely with the free man and the slave. It is not therefore the economic form of command that is naturalized against those who considered slavery a form of duress. Thanks to the shift accomplished by Aristotle, it is despotism that can now occupy the being of man as the authority of consciousness, in the name of an animal slavery that—at an earlier stage of the partition—corresponds to the animal's reduction to a mechanism lacking a soul (or 'à la mécanique ordinaire des corps bruts' [to the ordinary mechanics of the bare body] as Biran writes in the *Rapports du physique au moral*). In the meantime, the old paradigm of use must be reduced to that of command-activation (in such a way that the true instrument and the modern slave, the factory worker, becomes equivalent and interchange-able, according to the economic principle of exchange). In this sense,

19 Georges Canguilhem, *Knowledge of Life* (Paola Marrati and Todd Meyers eds, Stefanos Geroulanos and Daniela Ginsburg trans) (New York, NY: Fordham University Press, 2008), p. 84.

we could say that the syllogism is an enthymeme, but that the (Aristotelian, masterful) premise reveals its tautological circularity: because I think (because thought commands and uses, here in the restricted sense: *activates*) the body-mechanism, I think, therefore I am (the master of a body-instrument).

In Aristotle, the relation between soul and body is of an economic and despotic nature, just as the power exercised by the father over his property, his slaves and his instruments in the *oikos* is despotic and not political. What is political, in accordance with the definition of the human being as a *politikon zoon*, is the hierarchy within the soul, which subordinates the senses to the intellect, the irrational part to the rational one. In Descartes, however, the animal is a mechanical instrument that is subordinated to a being endowed with a soul: the man-animal distinction, that is, the definition of man as such, is no longer purely political in nature but first and foremost economic.

Now the 'I', the thinking subject, is a *pater familias* or landlord; now the model of economic despotism is the model of consciousness and therefore, of political consciousness especially. The reduction of the animal to a mechanical instrument (and its use for the activation thereof) has introduced man—now limited to his soul—into the domain of politico-economic sovereignty, that is to say, of an altogether novel corporeal slavery. Only such a shift could go on to make possible the interpretation that Karl Marx offers in *Capital*, where he recognizes the origin of executive and managerial labour, now autonomous from property and specific to the set-up of political economy, in the Aristotelian separation of dominion, which can be entrusted to supervisors, from properly philosophical and political affairs.[20]

It is on the basis of this borrowing or distortion, which is to say the economic definition of the animal and of mankind, that Descartes picks up the rule of the subordination of instinct to intellect. To recognize in his own way, after Aristotle, that an animal is incapable of judgement

20 Karl Marx, *Capital*, VOL. 3 (London: Electric Book Co., 2001), CHAP. 23, p. 512.

and lacks language, thereby denying it a political nature that it has never possessed, and conferring, on the other hand, the political being to the economic one. The politician and the master are united in a now-inextricable manner in the *je*, which thereby foreshadows the new slavery.

21. This is not the only matter at stake. And it would not suffice to return souls to animals to re-establish the classical distinction and restore the dream of an animate instrument and of natural possession. By now, there is no power that is coherent with the hierarchical man/animal or soul/body division that would be capable of commanding beings, things, or itself and therefore of re-establishing itself. And this is precisely because the new definition of the body, which concerns both the animate and inanimate, that is, its 'assimilation to a watch-mechanism', could not but irrevocably change the very modality of usage and dominion into a new and durable form that has spread everywhere, both among beings and things. 'Thus, in Descartes, the technological image of "command" (a type of positive causality by a device or by the play of mechanical connections) substitutes for the political image of commandment (a kind of magical causality; causality by word or by sign)'.[21]

As we have said, this new form of power corresponds to that of indubitability, that is, of the *cogito*. Once again: is it the form of a line of reasoning? Descartes seems to have implied as much, thus triggering that theory of questions (are we dealing with a perfect syllogism? Or an enthymeme? Or a paralogism?) that punctuates the history of philosophy from Gassendi to Régis, from Kant to Biran and the Hegelian affirmation of the *cogito*'s immediacy (*einfache Anschauung*), up to its twentieth-century interpreters. In the fundamental *Du rôle de l'idée de l'instant dans la philosophie de Descartes* (1920), the young Wahl admits that it would be possible to assign a form of reasoning to the *cogito . . . si l'on veut* and, in fact, as he would go on to specify in 1946 (*Tableau de la philosophie française*), this becomes necessary in the case of the slowest

21 Canguilhem, *Knowledge of Life*, p. 86.

of minds. It is still a form of reasoning, as Alquié insists again in 1955, capable (in the case of quicker minds, one might add) of grasping everything in a single instant:

> The 'I think therefore I am' is not the conclusion of a thought like 'in order to be one must think, now I am thinking, and therefore I am'. On the contrary, it is in the 'I think therefore I am' that the obviousness of the statement 'in order to think one must be' appears.

Everything, even if one is dealing with an enthymeme, originates in the pure form or in the quickness of intuition, in its concise nature ('there is no difference between Cartesian intuition and brief thought').

'Descartes's idealism is an actualism', Wahl continues: 'the *Cogito ergo sum* is therefore not a line of reasoning, although it can be translated into one [. . .] it is an intuition (*simplici mentis intuitu*) [. . .] it is the affirmation of an instantaneous certainty, it is a judgement, a thought condensed into an instant.'[22] Offering in the footsteps of his teachers an interpretation of the relation between doubt and intuition of the existence of God, or rather of the inseparability of the *cogito* from the ontological argument, Wahl condenses in the most rigorous of ways the perfect divine simultaneity and the synthetic actuality of the formula, i.e. 'la pensée finie en acte' (finite thought in action) and 'la pensée infinie en acte' (infinite thought in action).

But if Biran's effort is tied to the mortal body, the time of the *cogito* is thus granted and maintained (the *divina conservatio*) by a *vis* that consciousness cannot possess. Even actuality therefore reveals itself to Wahl in a fleeting and sinister light. Descartes, he remarks, often returns to the idea of life's brevity, and the extreme brevity of the *cogito* responds to the perils of infinite regression, that is, in essence, to death, which in the course of reasonings or deductions 'peut à tout moment me surprendre' (can surprise me at any moment).

---

22 Jean Wahl, *Du rôle de l'idée de l'instant dans la philosophie de Descartes* (Paris: Vrin, 1953[1920]), p. 5.

Before Pierre-Maxime Schuhl, it was Bréhier who, in a brief and important article in 1943, uncovered an Aristotelian precedent for the *cogito*. Following in the wake of the commentary by Alexander of Aphrodisia, while reading a passage of the *De sensu* ('when one has consciousness of one's self or of another person during a continuous period of time, one cannot at that time be unaware that one exists')[23] he noted that Aristotle already affirms the indissoluble union of self-perception and existence: exactly like Descartes, albeit 'with a singular and very important difference', Aristotle considers this union in a continuous time, taken as a single block, and deduces that it takes place at every moment, however small. 'By contrast, Descartes begins with the punctual and instantaneous evidence of the *cogito* which, with its repetition, creates duration'.[24]

Bréhier therefore did not limit himself to establishing a relation between the *cogito* and the Aristotelian source, but instead by comparing them highlighted the novelty and daring of Cartesian philosophy, based on a 'certitude évanouissante' (vanishing certainty). The fact that this interpretation was later brilliantly discussed and corrected by Rodolfo Mondolfo, who affirmed that the unions of consciousness and being already happened at specific time for Aristotle, confirms in its own way that persuasive actuality of the instantaneous *cogito*, which only a modern gaze, one that has so to speak been awoken by the Cartesian flash, could recognize in the dream of classical antiquity.

Thus, in the middle of the twentieth century, the diatribe initiated by Gassendi was once again resurrected, and right when these age-long questions seemed to be vanishing and the words of Descartes seemed to be attaining their utmost legibility. The understanding of the *cogito* was in fact suggested in many ways, to both challengers, and by the ever

23 Aristotle, *De sensu* in *De sensu and De memoria* (G. R. T. Ross trans.) (Cambridge: Cambridge University Press, 1906), p. 95 (448a).

24 Émile Bréhier, 'Une forme archaïque du cogito ergo sum', *Revue Philosophique de la France et de l'Étranger* 133(10–12) (1942–1943): 144.

more imperious figure of its correlate, the 'image technologique de "commande"' (technological image of command), which had in turn taken power as the great menace, ever capable of surprising with its incomparable speed. The most rudimentary concatenation could now trigger another equally rapid and unstoppable one, while the end of all duration, of the series of possible instants and conceptions, became in turn a matter of an instant.

The attention of philosophers had been captured precociously. Hardly a decade had passed since Wahl dedicated his essay on Descartes to Bergson when Gaston Bachelard wrote, in support of Gaston Roupnel and against Bergson, that 'time is the instant, and it is the present instant that bears the full weight of temporality'.[25] A new, radical theory of actuality had just made an appearance in Roupnel's novel *Siloë*, and by lending it a voice and developing it in an impassioned interpretation Bachelard anticipated in *Intuition de l'instant* (1931) the themes of *Dialectique de la durée* (1936) and of quantum scintillation first and foremost. This was the philosophy of discontinuous time that opposed the dominion of *durée* by defending punctual, unexpected and irreducible novelty and rejecting even the continuity of habit, now conceived of as a rhythm without duration. The positive evidence of the present thus appeared in the attention—as the *cogito* 'vide et solitaire' (empty and solitary) that 'ne dure pas' (does not last)—and in the decision, that is in their absolute or 'pré-initiale' (pre-initial) punctuality. Contemplating a cat lying in wait, Bachelard wrote, you will see 'l'*instant du mal*' (the *instant of evil*) inscribe itself in the real; certainly, the leap will occur in duration, but before the complicated process of the *élan* there is 'the simple and criminal instant of the decision'.

It was Albert Einstein's theory that awoke Bachelard from his dogmatic Bergsonism, revealing to him that there is no absolute duration. Even relativity, however, is still anchored in the preconception of a temporal *continuum*, and thus to Einstein's name one must also add that of

25 Gaston Bachelard, *Intuition of the Instant* (Eileen Rizo-Patron trans.) (Evanston, IL: Northwestern University Press, 2013), p. 28.

Max Planck, and to the equivalence of mass and energy the quantum theory of discrete values. At this point, however, the simplicity of the instant merged with the instantaneity of the decision as if in a grim portent, and the contemplative and prophetic gaze of the super-rationalist philosopher recognized in the flashing intention of the feline the numinous prestige of science. The truly pre-initial instant, the flash of radiation, had already inscribed itself onto the real, imposed 'the interesting comparison between the problem of the atom's positive existence and its ever-instantaneous manifestation'.

An apocalyptic light shines in the absolutely solitary headquarters, a pre-initial decision from which the economy of the animate being derives and on which it depends. And it is in this abbreviated time—in the last reduction of every development—that the syllogism once again finds in a new and concrete sense its intuitive quickness: 'It's enough to press a button, therefore I press it,' says Fritz Lang's Mabuse (*The Thousand Eyes of Dr Mabuse*, 1960). The mechanical activation of the mechanism: such is the definitive evidence of the *cogito* as a residual instantaneous act that is still attributable to an 'I'. The 'devaluation' of the living begun by Descartes reaches its fulfilment here.

22. Thus, in extreme brevity, duration and instant coincide. The notion of *effort* was perhaps the expression of a troubled presage, and therefore the attempt to hold back a time that had already expired, tying this coincidence to itself to make it continuous or, in turn, long-lasting. In the meantime, the famous premises and fruitful contradictions dictated by the Cartesian view matured: the punctuality of the present and the scholastic presupposition of divine *conservation* (originally renewed, as Hans Blumenberg has shown, in the theory of *creatio continua*), the thought without extension and its material burden, the idea and the image, dualism and with it the unity of the body and the soul, their conflation populated by intermediate animal spirits, justified by a singular materiality of the soul or conceived as a third substance, unassimilable to the two that coalesce in it. *Effort* was both the relation between these

opposites and, in its encounter with resistance, the conservation of the relation. It was both thought and diary: that is, a book written to ground not the 'I'-thing but even before that the *cogito* in the effort of writing, securing the latter and thus closing off time itself in a 'dated time preserved by its own date' (Maurice Blanchot).[26] And for this reason it was the most ambiguous of conquests, both long-lasting and ephemeral: it was the instant of a consciousness that continues because the body resists, and therefore under the threat of an irreducible exteriority precisely because it cannot last but must lose itself in sleep or death. Bréhier, one must remember, had shed light on this amphiboly, observing how the same term *effort*, which indicates a discontinuous, exceptional state or a brief interruption in the flux of thoughts, singularly designated in Biran a primitive fact present for the entire period during which there is consciousness, or in other words for the entire duration of the state of wakefulness.

In order to endure, the instantaneous punctuality of the act had to lean on the body, that is to say insist, distribute and transfer itself in the extension of its fibres, because the formula for the transformation of the instant into duration, or of the paradox of a residual and instantaneous duration, is a return-effect, a reaction, or a mutation of the force that becomes *effort* in its relation of intimacy with resistance. Bonnet already wrote, while explaining kinaesthetic sensation in terms that anticipated those of Maine de Biran,[27] that if the soul feels like it is moving an arm it is because the limb reacts to the brain. And it is precisely such a reaction that binds the Leibnizian force to the mortal body and prolongs the Cartesian instant in an already secondary time, as lasting as it is limited: the effort is the perceived force, which appears and defines itself only through resistance, and which when it appears is already a relatively constant 'fact' equal to itself (Bréhier).

26 Maurice Blanchot, *L'espace littéraire* (Paris: Gallimard, 1955), p. 20.

27 Jean Starobinski, *Action and Reaction: The Life and Adventures of a Couple* (Sophie Hawkes and Jeff Fort trans) (New York, NY: Zone Books, 2003), p. 123.

The vivacious Cartesian lymph thus generates a special, fruitful type of flowering. Certainly, the primitive fact as the origin of consciousness and the object of an immediate internal experience, or in other words the link between the two terms, is the nucleus of Biran's entire doctrine—from the criticism of Malebranche to the reading of Kant, from the theory of signs to that of the noumenal 'I' and to the ultimate reappearance, in a new and religious context, of the problem of the relation between the soul and the body (as Merleau-Ponty observed, 'on se retrouve au point de départ' [we find ourselves where we started])—but at least it is also the active and recognizable seed in the reading of Descartes offered by Fouillée. We think, as the philosopher of force-ideas observes, but *cogito* is already a word that we pronounce internally, knowing its sound, feeling a weak movement of the larynx. And even if our knowledge turned towards ourselves, if by achieving a divine and Aristotelian purity it became a thought of thought, it would still remain an attention to thought that 'ne va pas sans un *effort*': we would feel our muscles contract or our body's temperature go up, that is to say, our body manifest its presence.[28]

Opposing a thinker even as close and similar to him as Guyau, Fouillée perceived in the concept of 'vital sense' (*sentiment de la vie*) an overly-ambiguous intertwining of consciousness and kinaesthesia,[29] conceiving instead of an innate union of the mind and the body in consciousness itself; in other words, in the idea, understood as a unit of discernment and preference, an act that is conscious of its direction, intensity and quality, as the 'motor' of corporeal life, that is, as appetite and sensation in a nascent state. Thus, if Biran had accused Kant of not seeing the primitive fact, confusing effort with the first passive modification of sensibility, and had affirmed, ever since the *Influence de l'habitude sur la faculté de penser* (1799), that without internal resistance there

28 Fouillée, *Descartes*, pp. 105–6.

29 Alfred Fouillée, *La pensée et les nouvelles écoles anti-intellectualistes* (Paris: Alcan, 1911), p. 340.

could be no effort and without effort there could be no consciousness, in a different but corresponding manner Fouillée situated *effort* on the level of mental action (Bergson will later recognize it in the encounter with the resistance of problems, that is 'sur le trajet du schéma à l'image' [travelling from the scheme to the image]),[30] to affirm that every idea is already a choice, aimed at the satisfaction of our will and adverse to that which we hate, and that just as it can sense itself suffer or enjoy, the subject is conscious (in an immediate, pre-reflexive, non-objective consciousness) of his consent to pleasure or his refusal of pain. The will, or rather the force, thus binds the body to thought in thought itself and unites the *homo duplex* in a unique, non-contradictory tension. Before defending this position in front of his contemporaries (such as James or Paul Souriau), Fouillée had to necessarily defy the Kantian notion of vital force (*Lebenskraft*) from which, according to him, Schopenhauer's *Wille zum Leben* was directly derived. From his point of view, the force or the will has to essentially be foremost and free: against the *Anthropology from a Pragmatic Point of View* (§60), it must not depend on its opposite in the slightest. If indeed Kant takes inspiration from Pietro Verri to affirm that pleasure comes from pain, that the latter is always foremost, that the condition of health does not consist in the continuity of well-being but in its small inhibitions capable of promoting the vital force and of stimulating activity, and if he adds that in pain we sense life while only pleasure would extinguish it, Fouillée responds by saying that true pleasure is free from suffering, it is only a positive pleasure that immediately coincides with life and with force, which grows with the intensity of these two. This evidently means affirming that the force (or the will) tends towards life against pain and death. Fouillé must therefore still oppose to Verri and Kant the definition given by Bichat:

> La vie, a-t-on dit, est l'ensemble des forces qui résistent à la mort: la lutte pour vivre est continuelle. Le plaisir est la victoire,

30 Henri Bergson, *Mind-Energy: Lectures and Essays* (H. Wilden Carr trans.) (London: Macmillan, 1920), p. 166.

> la douleur est la défaite; le plaisir est la vie, la douleur est la mort.[31]

> (Life, it has been said, is the totality of forces that resist death: the struggle to live is continuous. Pleasure is victory; suffering is defeat; pleasure is life, suffering is death).

Man thus experiences and extends pleasure by opposing evil with all of his will and all of his ideas: his force is a resistance up until the end, that is played out, so to speak, before every thought. And if it is not necessarily and directly stimulated by pain, if it no longer has 'as its simple objective the preservation of the organism in the struggle for life', it is because it is already defined as such, as a 'plaisir direct' (direct pleasure), by its first antagonist, corporeal death. One could therefore infer that the energy of ideas or of the will that guides the mass of the living body is double, basilic, and political all at once, and that distinguishing and capturing the living being as a body whose afflictions it suffers and whose sensations it experiences, is the force of *some* ideas, precisely because it is also made of appetites or sense or—as one says—'of bile, of blood, of pituita, of flesh'.

The instant is therefore the time that death can surprise, it is the fatal instant, and its prolongation is a survival, it is the life that, in one interpretation or another, resists death in pleasure or passes through suffering, opposes it, and distinguishes from the former or through the latter. The basilic disposition of thought, the Cartesian hierarchy that governs the union of body and soul, is in other terms maintained by the inscription of the body in the continuous antagonism of pleasure and pain. But it is precisely this agon—the 'continuous production of vital force'—that is anthropological and in its own way political: the only body that the soul can govern—and therefore the modern definition of the psychosomatic individual, from Descartes to Kant, from Maine de Biran to Husserl—is both the result and the origin, the cause and the effect of a power-play that cannot be interrupted by an act of thought or

31 Alfred Fouillée, *La psychologie des idées-forces*, VOL. 1 (Paris: Alcan, 1893), p. 74.

by its possible material consequences, precisely because it is the *cogito* itself that establishes its economy. Force, which merely bonds the body and soul into a single individual, is the continuous product of the suffering body, which becomes ill, which lives for the lesser evil under the menace of the greater one in a duration that unwinds intuition into a syllogism so that it can be compressed again—closing off time itself within it—in a single millennium-like instant. Truly, in that case, 'the *ergo* cannot mean "consequently" '.[32]

. . . Philosophy itself becomes a self-witnessing and an art of living that is always bitter and at the same time oriented towards the sunset and lined with sadness, because all that we can truly know of it we will only know 'quand il est temps *de* mourir' (*when it is* time *to* die). *In the meantime, the will, habit, freedom, private and social life harken back to the fundamental duplicity that binds force to its opposite: the act of thinking intersects with unconscious life, it keeps an* ergo *with no continuation in an instant that is both prolonged and brief, projecting its own effort on the level of mental states and of all thoughts. And this closure—this biological bond—of temporality is a type of governance, that produces and contains its subjects by anchoring itself in the basilic despotism of the soul over the body and by spreading it, according to the gradation of temperaments, characters, personalities, from the intimacy of the effort to the entirety of society, from* compos sui *to the state of somnambulism, from the retreat of Grateloup to the highest levels of society and thus from that centre to all of Paris and finally back to and beyond Grateloup.*

While Leibniz's and Descartes's point de vue ontologique *was traced by Biran back to the* fait primitif, *it marked the convergence of anthropology and psychology. And if every idea belonging to man contains and imposes a political concept, the latter can later be isolated or dispersed, or activated in a series of secondary and in turn psychological efforts . . .*

32 Heidegger, *Nihilism*, p. 113.

V

Property

23. 'Thus each organic body of a living thing is a kind of divine machine, or natural automaton, which infinitely surpasses all artificial automata.'[1] Just as the dominating actuality of the cogito is inseparable from the reduction of the animal to a machine, so the distinction between the latter and the organism, between the operation of the soul (the spiritual automaton) and the mechanism are also the bulwarks of Leibniz's theory of the soul's dominion over the body, informed by the *consensus* or—to use the formula from the preface to the *Nouveaux essais sur l'entendement humain*—by the 'admirable harmonie préétablie' (admirable pre-established harmony). If living bodies are machines in their smallest details and thus *ad infinitum*, the soul as a superior entelechy has a body that is made of infinite monads, each of which has its own principal entelechy. A divine machine, a living automaton composed of an infinity of living beings, the body is not therefore the stable dominion of the soul, as if the latter were the owner of 'other inferior living things which are forever destined to serve it'.[2] There is in fact no long-lasting and unalterable possession because the body is not an inert mass; rather, it is indestructible like the river that remains the same while everything in its bed flows and changes. As Leibniz says, the river flows and the entelechy remains, and so the machine subsists. According to the pre-established

1 Gottfried Wilhelm Leibniz, *Leibniz's Monadology: A New Translation And Guide* (Lloyd Strickland trans.) (Edinburgh: Edinburgh University Press, 2014), §64.

2 *Leibniz's Monadology*, §71.

harmony, from the beginning to the end of the world, body and soul harmonize according to their own individual laws, they unite while maintaining their autonomous lives and influence each other without contradicting their reciprocal independence.

Now, Leibniz had to guarantee for all monads the metaphysical unity that formally constitutes composite substances, conferring to the hierarchic relation between the dominating monad and the innumerable others a spontaneity that was still unknown to Cartesian automatism and mechanism. After the initial difficulties, having abandoned the attempt to define a quasi-substance, he was able to coin—in 1712, while writing to Barthélemy Des Bosses—the notion of the *vinculum substantiale*. This singular concept, which was to provoke firm objections from the Jesuit theologian, would later go on to pique Biran's interest, before falling into a lengthy oblivion. It would in fact go on to be reduced for the entire duration of the nineteenth century by the authoritative voices of Robert von Zimmermann, Heinrich Ritter, Eduard Zelle and Wilhelm Windelband to a sophistic accommodation or a diplomatic concession to the Catholic dogma of transubstantiation. This restrictive reading would last at least until Bertrand Russell's *Critical Exposition of the Philosophy of Leibniz* (1900). It is only Maurice Blondel who, from an anti-Kantian perspective (in his doctoral thesis from 1893, revised and published in 1930) and later the historian Alfred Boehm (1938), so attentive to the relations between seventeenth-century scholasticism and modern philosophy, who will break the general silence of exegetes, restoring the late resolving hypothesis to its role as the 'couronnement "exigé"' ('demanded' crowning) of Leibniz's philosophy.[3] In Blondel's interpretation, the *vinculum* is the true bond of every fragment and also the keystone, the 'fissure secrète' (secret fissure) of the monadologic system, which welds the new theory of substance with the Aristotelianism of the *vis primitiva et insita*. By introducing into his metaphysics of force

3 Maurice Blondel, *Une énigme historique*: *Le 'Vinculum Substantiale' d'après Leibniz et l'ébauche d'un réalisme supérieur* (Paris: Beauchesne, 1930), p. 125.

a theoretically disconcerting notion and conferring on it a name apparently marked by passivity, and therefore 'inattendu et énigmatique' (unexpected and enigmatic),[4] Leibniz had in fact conceived of the aggregate of composites not as a simple relation but as an intrinsic and active unity, *componens et uniens, as a* 'res unionalis' or a substance in itself. Only this independent and *uniens quid* could in fact maintain the *consensus* and that very independence of monads, tying them into a single body and at the same time binding the dominating entelechy to the innumerable monads of the organism, and thus the soul to the body, the constant term to the mutable one. Reading the epistolary exchange between Leibniz and Des Bosses in the wake of the late-Aristotelian theory by Francisco Murcia de la Llana, Boehm insisted on the fact that the *vinculum* entertains a special relation of adherence—and not inherence—to the monads. That is, its reality does not intimately compenetrate the being it unites with, but entertains with them a relation that could be defined as one of external intimacy. As Leibniz explained to Des Bosses, the *vinculum* physically depends or rather *demands* the existence of monads (without which it could not carry out its role) while remaining metaphysically unconditioned by it ('Vinculum substantiale, etsi naturaliter seu physice exigat monades, quia tamen non est in illis tamquam in subiecto, non requiret eas metaphysice'), 'because it is not inherent in them as a subject and it can subsist, identical to itself, when they are substituted by other monads.'[5] A substance in and of itself, both transcendent and immanent with respect to the composite substance onto which it confers existence, the tie is thus, to use Deleuze's words, 'a strange bond, a hook, a yoke, a knot' which, by adhering without inhering, ensures the independence of the body and the soul while uniting them in a complex and unstable relation of appropriation. It is only thanks to this third party that subsists on its own that the *conatus* can in fact remain virtual without ceasing to act, while the appropriation does

4 Blondel, *Une énigme historique*, p. 32.

5 Alfred Boehm, *Le 'Vinculum substantiale' chez Leibniz: Ses origines historiques* (Paris: Vrin, 1938), p. 115.

not reduce one term to the other but installs between the two a relation that is in turn lively and changeable. It is only thanks to the *vinculum* that the property of the soul is not an attribute thereof, or an inert extension, but the body as the precarious aggregate of mutable monads. If the soul thus has a body, and has had it since the beginning of time, this having, as Deleuze has observed, does not introduce a placid continuity of stable possession once and for all. The true successor of Leibniz is therefore Gabriel Tarde—capable of developing monadology both into a universal sociologism and into a philosophy of having whereby every phenomenon is an association of various beings and phenomena, of recognizing that that which is dominant in the monad is precisely a having. Indeed, from a radically Leibnizian point of view, the constancy of the domination is nothing but an inexhaustible and ever mutable possession: the natural automaton, an association or amalgam of an infinite number of natural automata, a body possessed that continues to flow and change, and never ceases to bind itself to him who will never be able to *be* its proprietor because, ever possessing something different, he will only ever be able to *have*. If the inventory of possession changes infinitely, if one possesses a body that increases and decreases incessantly, no property will ever be able to be or hypostatize itself in a being. In Tarde's words, 'At the basis of every notion of being, there is the notion of having. But the inverse is not true, either: being is not the entire content of the idea of possession.'[6] The body teeming with monads of the pre-established harmony does not require an ontology but a new knowledge for which 'j'ai' (I have) is the 'fait fondamental' (fundamental fact). It will teach that having is infinite, that its list does not end, that the constant term, the dominating monad, is continuously dealing with its mutable body. In other words, the notion of having as an occupation or a reciprocal grasp implies a counter-blow or a counter-possession. It is precisely the dominion that never ceases to exercise itself that will never be univocal:

6 Gabriel Tarde, *Monadologie et sociologie*, Œuvres de Gabriel Tarde, VOL. 1 (Éric Alliez pres. and Maurizio Lazzarato postf.) (Le Plessis-Robinson: Institut Synthélabo pour le progrès de la connaissance, 1999[1893]), p. 87.

'Unilateral and reciprocal possession [. . .] are [. . .] necessarily united', Tarde explains, specifying with typical Leibnizian rigour that 'the latter is superior to the former.'[7] If the possession is harmonious, the harmony is a hierarchy, a hierarchy deprived of ontological stability. Tied to one another by the *vinculum substantiale*, the monads can belong to each other in differing degrees and manners, and therefore they transform in turn, differentiating themselves continuously while every form of even elementary and direct domination, such as that between a master and a slave, mutates and amplifies, becomes more complicated, multiplies and silently inverts, not via a dialectical overturning, not because 'the equality of right, popular sovereignty and the equal exchange of services' occurs, but *precisely because it endures*, where difference reigns, on the infinite spectrum of what is discernible, where one cannot 'be a proprietor' if being, in turn, means always having differently.

True heir of Leibniz's that he was, Tarde was both an admiring and a critical reader of Maine de Biran. In cases where the 'donc j'ai' (therefore I have) replaces the 'donc je suis' (therefore I am), no *effort* will indeed be able to force consciousness into existence. Thus, the phrase 'in society I am a somnambulist' which in Biran's work defined the negative condition of being lost, the loss of will and consciousness, the end of self-mastery, acquires precisely the opposite meaning in Tarde. If everything for the philosophy of having is social, if every phenomenon is an association of phenomena, society itself is *une espèce de somnambulisme*[8] and indeed one of the happiest of them all: 'the reciprocal possession, in extremely varied form, of everyone by everyone'.[9] If this inversion is possible, if passivity (of the magnetized) is not a defeat, it is precisely because the punctual instantaneity of the *sum* and the actuality of the effort that had to maintain it are replaced by the infinite play of differences. When the *j'ai* expresses the apperception of the different degrees

7 Tarde, *Monadologie et sociologie*, p. 92.

8 Gabriel Tarde, 'Qu'est-ce qu'une société?', *Revue Philosophique de la France et de l'Étranger* 18 (1884): 509.

9 Tarde, *Monadologie et sociologie*, p. 85.

and variable conditions of property, the Biranian 'fact' reveals itself to be the product of a singular illusion: indeed, 'without a recollection of the previous distinct, or discernible, or mutated states, we would not have the apperception of the current state as such, as real.'[10] Having therefore replaces being when the Leibnizian conception of time dethrones the intuition of the instant. Thus, for Tarde, death consists in the reduction or in the return to the infinitesimal of the element that, in the course of imitations, had arisen from its first obscure condition to become dominant. It is not the nothingness beyond life, or another life, but *non-life*, that is, a different modality of existence in which monads, having been restored to their originality, definitively and painlessly renounce corporeal desires. And perhaps the first life was nothing but an imposed exercise so that, 'leaving this hard and mystical school', they could find themselves 'purified by the earlier need for universal domination.'[11] They will then be freed from evil just as they will be freed of regrets for that 'cerebral throne' or 'corporeal power' to which they happily abdicated.

Thus, death, which demanded explanations, is given value, while life obtains in exchange a justification. And in the new theatre of Tarde's harmony there will only be one true act, 'eternally lasting', before which there is only a 'time of rehearsals'. But here there are no actors, one cannot see an audience, and even the faintest of scenarios is missing. It is only by allowing himself a conclusive 'débauche métaphysique' (metaphysical debauchery) that Tarde can at least imagine that 'divine condition' in which 'the last second of life' introduces the monads, which begins and develops beyond the possession of the body. Rather, he *must* imagine it, before the fatal instant, in the evident and unilateral force of that property and that power.

10 Gabriel Tarde, *Maine de Biran et l'évolutionnisme en psychologie* (Éric Alliez fore. and Anne Devarieux pref.) (Paris: Institut d'édition Sanofi-Synthélabo, 2000[1876]), p. 76.

11 Tarde, *Monadologie et sociologie*, p. 102.

24. According to Canguilhem, who discusses Marxist interpretations, Descartes integrated a 'phénomène humain' (human phenomenon) into his philosophy, the building of machines, more than he transposed a social phenomenon—capitalist production—into ideology. According to Deleuze, on the other hand, Leibniz's metaphysics are related, like all of the Baroque, to a crisis of property that explodes with the introduction and development of new mechanisms in the social sphere, along with the discovery of new living beings inside the organism. Descartes was interested in clocks, windlasses and contraptions meant for lifting weights, in water mills and the dynamics of projectiles. But when a product of the inventive spirit such as the microscope assumes the role of a protagonist, there is no longer any 'human phenomenon'—one might gloss—that can appear foreign, due to an old or presumed purity, to the history of economic structures and their crises.

The Cartesian reduction of the animal organism to a machine did indeed found—in the instantaneous coincidence of being and thought—a form of dominion that Leibniz's influence would have impeded, giving rise to the minor current of universal socio-morphism and to the philosophy of having. Other more evident tensions would later propagate from the laboratory of preformist theories, via the diatribes of doctors, naturalists and philosophers, and by following the man/animal partition would go on to produce new shake-ups and distinctions in the already-unstable dominion of the person and of consciousness. Bonnet's position has already been mentioned, but not that of his pointed critic, Cabanis's fierce opponent, Frédéric Bérard, one of the last great masters of the School of Montpellier, who, in 1823, affirmed that an animal senses and unites its sensations in its consciousness, and therefore possesses an 'I', a principle of unity or a sort of soul, although, as Bonnet himself believed, it may have 'only a vague, limited, unreflective sentiment of its own personality'.[12] Thus, a new intensity had been attained, which can be found

12 Frédéric Bérard, *Doctrine des rapports du physique et du moral: Pour servir de fondement à la métaphysique, à la physiologie dite intellectuelle et à la métaphysique* (Paris: Gabon et Compagnie, 1823), p. 607.

verbatim in a worried comment made by Maine be Biran: 'Ce qui est l'extrême opposé à Descartes, *que je préférerais qu'il fallait*' (Which is the complete opposite of Descartes, which I would prefer).[13] And he would have certainly preferred it, just as he would have preferred that living or acting 'in society' not necessitate giving up the calm concentration granted by Grateloup, that is to say of the certainty of one's own being, or that the somnambular voices and airs of the capital not come disturb that mastery which had been won with such difficulty: 'I was born to live in that happy time of the monarchy', he wrote in January of 1816, in the time of Louis XVIII and of the 'Chambre introuvable' (unfindable room), 'in which Malebranche, Arnault, Leibniz, Pascal [. . .] offered so many exercises for the meditative faculty!'[14]

Si Leibniz avait été psychologue . . . The title with which Gouhier sums up Biran's reading of the 'grand maître' (great teacher) finds its direct equivalent here: if Biran had lived in the happy times of Leibniz . . . then the principle of entelechy would have appeared alongside its origin and the point of view of the *moi* would not have become confused with the divine one. But happy psychology and happy monarchy never got the chance to meet. Marked thus by nostalgia and by a yearning for an ideal restoration, Biran's philosophy comes forth in the admirable attempt to formulate a Leibnizian theory of the *je suis* by tying a *force* that has become estranged from the pre-established harmony to the time and being of consciousness. In its own way, this is a radical philosophy of property and of property as being, or better yet of possession that *wishes* to be stable, thus requiring a constant effort. In a manner that is only initially surprising, this stability of what is one's own, the fixity of the I-thing and of being, therefore coincides with the effort or bears within it the marker of discontinuity. If property is not virtual, the *conatus* must necessarily imprint itself on the resisting body.

---

13 Maine de Biran, *Nouveaux essais d'anthropologie*, p. 35.

14 Maine de Biran, *Journal*, VOL. 1, p. 102.

25. The primacy of ontology must be re-established, and that precisely where a philosophy of pure having can now affirm itself. In another page of his diary, from March 1817, Biran encounters Locke's principle ('Ever Man has a Property in his own Person'), reflecting on the idea, on the origin of property, and on the words of his friend André Morellet:

> Property, possession, is both a distinct term and a correlate of a subject that has or *possesses*. We rightly say that a man is in possession of his senses, that he is *compos sui*. Now, this is not certain because he is merely living or *sentient*: we cannot say that a man is in full possession of himself or *compus sui* because he forms a *totality*, a system composed of different *organs*. On the contrary, the more alive his senses are, the more he finds himself in this state of *passion* that is accompanied by the greatest *activity* possible, from a psychological and objective point of view, and the less a man is in possession of himself, the less consciousness or *compos sui* he has.
>
> I too, like the Abbot Morellet, believe that we must seek out the foundation of property or of the idea of property in the *I* of man. First, however, we must know what is understood by the word *I* and go back to the origins of individual personality. We will not find this origin in the mixture of the living, the organic, the sentient, but rather in the simple being that acts or generates the effort and that *disposes* of a few of the faculty of that same complex.[15]

Tied to personality, naturally unknown to animals ('Un être passif et purement sensitif, n'ayant pas la conscience du *moi* ou n'étant pas une *personne*, ne saurait avoir une telle idée' [A passive and purely sensitive being, one lacking a consciousness of the *I* or not constituting a *person*, could not have such an idea]), property orders the world of human privileges, unfolds in juridical freedoms while immanent effort prolongs itself through work:

15 Maine de Biran, *Journal*, VOL. 2, p. 25.

> Arising from the immediate sensation of the body's property, moved by the will and in general by all of the faculties available for the exercise or our free activity, the idea of the law of property extends to all of the external products of this activity, to every result of our effort, of a voluntary *work* that is like a part of ourselves.

And once again, with a phrase that harkens back to an old rudiment of law and which will be punctually repeated by Pierre Janet:[16] 'We are wounded in this external property when it is attacked, just as we would be in our very own person.'[17]

Thus, both in the definition of the individual subject ('Il faut bien savoir ce qu'on doit entendre par le *moi*' [we must well understand what it is that we mean by the *I*]) and of personality ('et remonter jusqu'à l'origine de la personalité' [and go back to the origins of personality]), what is at stake is the same material possession. In the *effort*, the latter is tied to being just as being remains tied to property, according to a double implication of which the term 'person' now provides a concise expression. And the clearest definition of this bond appears unsurprisingly from the negative point of view of an offence against property which is at the same time an offence against the subjectivity of the proprietor. While remaining grounded in the lengthy juridical history of the *diminutio* of an individual as the loss of a title or social rank or property, such a conception essentially distinguishes itself from that of pure having, which knows neither offences nor losses but only new unfoldings or in other words new and more subtle developments. When it is tied to an individual being, property becomes exposed to injury and aggression, and the exposure is so primary, its nature is shaken to such an extent, that it will notoriously have to reveal itself, in turn, as theft. Indeed, only there, where possession and subjective existence coincide, where property is personal or private, nothing can affirm itself or last if not at the expense

16 Pierre Janet, *De l'angoisse à l'extase: Études sur les croyances et les sentiments*, VOL. 2: *Les sentiments fondamentaux* (Paris: Félix Alcan, 1928), pp. 54–55.

17 Maine de Biran, *Journal*, VOL. 2, pp. 25–26.

of what is one's own. And so it is for life: wherever it resists death, that is to say its negative correlative, it opposes itself once again only to life. Here, antagonism reigns, every effort is like Sisyphus's effort and the two principles—of life and property—unite in the individual person, a closed form designed to defend weak borders, which both rejects and ends in privation and death.

26. But if the identity of the *effort* coincides with the identity of the personal being it is the problem of the relation between continuity and discontinuity that must be resolved. As François Azouvi notes, Biran based the apperception of temporal continuity on corporeal spatiality in an original fashion, thus succeeding in retaining the immediacy of the instantaneous relation of the I-cause to the movement-effect. He came up with this solution while revisiting the *Essai sur la décomposition de la pensée* in 1805, to then develop it two years later in the *Aperception immédiate* and later in the *Essai sur les fondements de la psychologie* (1812). 'The single development of this common effort, the uniformity or continuity of organic resistance', Biran writes, 'must correspond to the sense of a sort of initially vague and unlimited *interior extension*'. The instantaneous effort is thus the initial position of the 'I', the origin of time and simultaneously the apperception of the 'internal and unlimited space of one's own body'. Now, precisely this space, which corresponds in a certain sense to the corporeal imprint of the effort, is not objective, fixed or measurable, but—ever since there is time, ever since an 'I' endures—progressively uncovered and grasped, according to ever-more subtle distinctions that correspond to single voluntary acts. Continuity is thus assured, the apperception that serves as the basis for time becomes ever clearer, 'the motor subject is individualized more completely',[18] or rather, according to Daniel Heller-Roazen's keen observation, the 'I' gradually distinguishes itself from the internal space from which it can never free itself entirely, revealing thus the gap that divides

18 Maine de Biran, *Of Immediate Apperception*, p. 108; see Azouvi, *Maine de Biran*, p. 239.

it from its substrate, the unbridgeable difference between the perceiver and the perceived.[19] The story of the figure that we ourselves are is therefore enclosed in this impossibility of coinciding with one's own backdrop. As with the art of living, one could indeed also observe regarding corporeal spatiality that 'on ne le connaît guère que quand il *est temps* de *mourir*' (but we only come to know it when it is *time to die*). Only in the death of the body can individuality truly call itself that—personal.

One thus reaches the primitive and insuperable amphiboly that constitutes both the foundation and at the same time the mythical character of the property or identity of a person. The ambiguity is a primary one, for it is the spectre of the end that constitutes what is one's own as such every time, grounding the effort in corporeal spatiality. It is in the name of the 'eternal enemy' or of the untiring threat that property is maintained for the long-lasting instant of the *effort*—and can therefore disguise as its own a continuity that does not belong to it and that is at its adversary's disposal. And it is under the simultaneously hostile and complicit gaze of such a gorgon that Biran can pronounce his 'je ne deviens pas, réellement et absolument je suis' (I do not become; truly and absolutely, I am). Where intimidation reigns, it is consciousness itself that does not develop and that, blocked in its *croyance*, attributes its own fixity to the 'I'. Personality (property) can therefore transform (first, second . . . sane, infirm) precisely because it remains excluded from becoming, that is, in the absolute and real manner of a thing that replaces another, because its own being coincides with its state, with the gravity or resistance that, in changing, transforms the philosopher and writer into a Parisian somnambulist. Precisely for the same reason, however, precisely because physical death threatens and nullifies every effort, consciousness can never cease to distinguish itself from the body, and property (personality) is never definitive if not, paradoxically, in its subtraction, in the single instant of its undoing.

19 Daniel Heller-Roazen, *The Inner Touch: Archaeology of a Sensation* (New York: Zone Books, 2007), p. 235.

Let us recall then Merleau-Ponty's precise formula: Biran 'foresaw a spatiality of the body prior to objective spatiality, a presence of the outside world within the consciousness of the self'.[20] This exteriority—one must add—precedes any objectivity by remaining ungraspable, since its true, full or impossible presence would only be an absence of force and life. Consciousness is therefore consciousness and appropriation of the only entity that can belong to it and at the same time of the only entity that, by definition, never ceases to elude it. Such is the structure of property, which is in itself ambiguous and contradictory but nevertheless real and efficient. Yes, property is a theft because it is death that assigns it and takes it away, and he who pretends to have it is actually stealing it from its most legitimate and mysterious owner. Thief and owner coincide and perhaps this coincidence marks the modern origin of the right of property and of the rights of a person.

Once again, we witness an inversion and an effect of return: the spatial *continuum* resolves the temporal discontinuity and transforms every instant into the fraction of a single activity of distinction or appropriation (both of the organs and of the conscious 'I'). But it is precisely for this reason that the shadow of death pervades at every instant the continuity of bodies or days, which remains vague and indefinite like the spectre that hovers over it.

Thus, personality lays the foundations for property by reflecting and tying being to uncertainty itself: and once one presumes to come to the end of the latter (since it is the most difficult to endure) by overturning it into its apparent opposite (its correlative), thus evoking—like Heidegger, in §52 of *Sein und Zeit*—the certainty (*Gewißheit*) of death to magically transform life into the only possible being-certain (*Gewiß*sein)[21]—as if the absolutely certain had to be certainly possible or foreseeable—one will only obtain a world of death where death dominates because uncertainty is called destiny. The 'peut à tout moment me surprendre' (can surprise us at any moment) does not cease at any rate

20 Merleau-Ponty, *Incarnate Subject*, p. 75.

21 Martin Heidegger, *Being and Time* (Joan Stambaugh trans.) (New York, NY: State University of New York Press, 1996), p. 238.

to reflect onto the world, from a centre and from a time that have just been conquered. And now everything, outside, appears already present, reflects and relaunches the instant of the act of consciousness, which cannot situate itself in time if not on the basis of a reflexive chronology, itself objective and exterior. And it is to this derived objectivity that the body and the ego itself should supposedly belong.

Merleau-Ponty once again noted in his own way this movement of returning, reproaching Maine de Biran, the recognized precursor of phenomenology, with a fall into psychologism: all while rooting the 'I' in the body, the latter assumes the point of view, which is no longer philosophical but precisely psychological, of the external observer, which treats it as something explainable. The criticism is illuminating. But—remembering that very same 'psychological conversation' with Morellet—it must be slightly corrected: it is not due to an incoherence or a lack, but precisely because of the tie to the body that the Biranian subject is forced to divide himself, and to contemplate himself from a perspective that is a good deal more naive than that of the Husserlian *Ichspaltung*. After Merleau-Ponty, others have thought to see a defect or an inadequacy in the Biranian notion of the body. A notion, as has been said, inherited from his eighteenth-century masters and taken up without any innovation, which later, it has been said, impeded the development of a true phenomenology of corporeal intentionalities; a concept recovered from an old arsenal, which would have required a radical theoretical re-elaboration, if it did not find itself in a singular correspondence with the physical condition of the philosopher.

> Whether it was about Rousseau or Bonnet, the Idéologues (and especially Cabanis) or the psychologists of his time, Biran always found psycho-physiological explanatory schemas which he adopted not so much as a result of their intrinsic theoretical value, as much as because of the painful persistence of an experience with which they seemed to match up.[22]

22 Michel Henry, *Philosophie et phénoménologie du corps: Essai sur l'ontologie biranienne* (Paris: Presses Universitaires de France, 1965), pp. 214–15.

If there has ever been a psycho-physiological explanation, one might say, then it is precisely this one given by Michel Henry. It finds itself echoed in the words with which Xavier Tilliette hints at the possible origins of the philosophy of the intimate fact: 'Like Rousseau, the pre-romantic, the inconstant Biran, subject to the fluctuations of a melancholic temperament, invokes this happiness . . . that dispenses a sweet and immobile *rêverie*. But when he emerges from this ecstasy, he speaks of a "return to oneself" '.[23] While we cannot agree with these interpretations, nevertheless we cannot fail to recognize that, under different angles, they grasp a singular trait, they mark the exchange between the external and the internal, the continuous oscillation of the observer's position: when the world is wholly marked by the uncertainty of personality, it now includes the body and the *effort* or the personality itself, and the mournfulness becomes a second, insuperable consciousness which from the world returns to the internal effort all without ceasing to disperse it in the exteriority of the world. Property does not become but is, and in its being it does not fulfil itself but rather separates from itself in a melancholy vision.

27. 'The patient, it would seem, has an extra personality, he believes himself to be another and says precisely: "I am another"; which of course leave many surprised because in speaking thus he says "I"'.[24] The words used by Tarde regarding Taine and Krishaber's cerebro-cardiac neuropathy are reminiscent of Lignac's argument against Descartes: the certainty of one's own existence is 'renfermée dans le mot *je*' (enclosed in the word I). But what draws together the linguistic sign and consciousness as properties of the self?

Biran also of course borrows the semantic theory from the Idéologues to nevertheless impress upon it the original inflection of appropriation or of the primitive fact. He thus explains that in his infantile and purely

23 Xavier Tilliette, 'Nouvelles réflexions sur le Cogito biranien', *Revue de Métaphysique et de Morale* 88(4) (1983): 439.

24 Tarde, *Maine de Biran et l'évolutionnisme en psychologie*, pp. 55–56.

sensitive existence, the child emits sounds that only constitute 'a sort of language' for his nurse, who is capable of understanding them as the signs of various affects. It is only when he grows and becomes a person, only in that precise moment, does the child perceive those inarticulate cries as the first purposeless movements, and repeats them voluntarily, thus conferring on them intention and meaning for the first time. A signifying phoneme is a phoneme that is at least repeated and the word *lallatio* says for speech what Henry Michaux has written about children's first drawings: 'Au commencement est la / RÉPÉTITION' (In the beginning is REPETITION).[25] It is in repetition, by closing the first circles or pursuing the voice, that the child 'appropriates indefinite movements as an acting person and institutes them thus as *signs*'. The articulation of sound therefore completes the definition of consciousness that develops and distinguishes itself from that which moves, while as sign, in every single conquest of sound, the vague and internal space of the sensitive body extends itself into exteriority. Appropriation and pronunciation, consciousness and property of language, apperception as the possessive retaking of the voice . . . it is once again property that spreads through its signs . . . But at the same time repetition reigns as the inscription of what is one's own in exteriority, as the conquest and simultaneous scission of the *je* into observer and observed, both 'I' and other at the same time, as the immediate entrance of that 'je suis' (I am) into a world in which he will henceforth be accompanied by 'René Descartes', or the communication of what is one's own that spreads as a sign-thing in the world of objects, as the dissipation of what is one's own and the reflection of the external sign on the body, or as the border of property which expands in signs and exposes itself to the attack of signs, to the implacable workings of the world (of Paris) which conquers the internal effort. *Compos sui, compos linguae* . . . an appropriation that already pursues itself in the pages and in the fleeting ambiguity of the diary, while, having always had to communicate it, it releases the 'je suis' out into the world of signs

---

25 Henri Michaux, *Les commencements: Dessins d'enfants, essais d'enfant* (Montpellier: Fata Morgana, 1983), p. 8.

but only to be able to repeat it anew, to pronounce or write it once more. And in the meantime, the daily count of the properties that are about to leave us, and that will leave us when they are truly ours continues, when the person will be able to call himself one with a sound both definitive and unrepeatable. Let us recall here, with Jean Fallot, and even before that with Marcel Proust, the regret experienced by the cardinal Mazarin while looking at his books and paintings, all that he would have to abandon: we remember him not only because this last glance would also end up in a book, a diary, precisely, to which one's eyes are still turned, but also because precisely in that scared and melancholy tonality the same force or the same power resounds that in repeating the word personifies itself. In language there echoes a primary 'je suis', implicit and reclaimed in every sign as the formula of appropriation. Born of the sentiment of the body's property, the law can then name its external products: and if it is a sign ('Cartesius') or fact of language that ties being to its properties, the juridical intertwining of being and language is in turn tied together by property. And in this situation in which the thief and the owner coincide, the same power that offers protection can threaten, belittle, deprive and deny personality.

28. From Descartes to Biran, the road that leads from pure thought to being passes through property and discovers in *effort* the constitutive instant of the person and of every right, and therefore declares that the sign, the word, is the expression both of the effort and of the juridical bond. Thus, property besieges thought, which is now in the hands of language. One may think back to Stirner: 'Language or "the word" tyrannizes hardest over us, because it brings up against us a whole army of *fixed ideas*'.[26] And along with Stirner one might remember Marx: in the *Unico*, the presupposition of the possessor reigns, there is the strongest faith in the will, and at the end one only finds 'the simple statement of personal identity'. But that is precisely where the greatness of the book

---

26 Stirner, *Ego and Its Own*, p. 305.

lies, and even the most implacable criticism can serve as an advantage for its objective. Stirner limited himself to the most immediate evidence, without realizing that in the era of competition, 'personality is mere chance, and mere chance is personality'. But in the dominion of chance, that is to say in the dominion of mythological projections, even a mere constatation becomes an arduous undertaking: it implies an excess, and perhaps reaching it means overcoming it. To trace having back to being is in fact the properly juridical act: it founds and renews the law and the state of security as a continual defence of a property that, being originally uncertain, 'must be respected'. By contrast, tracing property back to individuality or individuality to pure property, that is, thinking property in an absolute sense, is the act that demands the destruction of the law and of the State.

One may also recall Marx's irony: 'If "Stirner" passes by the royal kitchen, he will undoubtedly acquire possession of the smell of the pheasants roasting there, but he will not even see the pheasants themselves. The only persisting possession that falls to his share is a more or less vociferous rumbling in his stomach'.[27] The sarcasm is brilliant, but look at its target: 'it is [. . .] *my* fibres that quiver under the blows, and *I* moan because *my* body moans. That *I* sigh and shiver proves that I have not yet lost *myself*, that I am still my own'.[28] Such is the affirmation of *compos sui*: here, truly, personality, or the being of the proprietor, 'identifies itself with its body, so that it is wholly "its own", outwardly as well as inwardly, so long as it still retains a spark of life, even if it is merely unconscious life.'[29] But it is equally true that up until then I remain purely *mine*, even if 'the fetters of reality cut the sharpest welts in my flesh'.[30] The paradox is a serious one and here, truly, in its affirmation, personality, by identifying itself with the body, by driving itself

27 Karl Marx, 'Saint Max' in *The German Ideology*, VOL. 1 (Amherst, NY: Prometheus, 1998), p. 312.

28 Stirner, *Ego and Its Own*, p. 143.

29 Marx, 'Saint Max', pp. 325–26.

30 Stirner, *Ego and Its Own*, p. 143.

beyond consciousness, or in other words beyond its object, possesses only itself, it both 'belongs to itself' and is 'the proprietor of itself'. Perhaps it is not just hunger that is long-lasting, as in Marx's parody: it is instead only the possession of myself as the possessor, the pure unsatisfied possession that remains in privation as a naked *power of having*, as having that is not the acquisition of something, of this or that ever precariously present object. 'My property', this having nothing but having, which is not abstract because it owes nothing to the concrete, this truly intact property that is un-subtractable, coincides with an equally pure hunger, it reigns precisely in the absence of the thing or in the void of being: 'my property is not a thing, since this has an existence independent of me; only my might (*Gewalt*) is my own. Not this tree, but my might or control over it, is what is mine'.[31] If in Maine de Biran's view, privation or poverty was a wound inflicted on a person, now the person coincides with the wound itself and outdoes the substantial integrity of the body in a pure and simple *mine*; and it escapes its own being when it grasps itself, and as having without being it makes itself into a power over property-being via the simple loss of any consideration: 'I do not step shyly back from your property, but look upon it always as *my* property, in which I need to 'respect' nothing. Pray do the like with what you call my property!'[32] This strange subject, this 'person' as a mask of property or of the chance that decides it, is not founded on the appropriating repetition of language or on the reflexive instantiation of speech (*je*), which fixes thought to signs and to the law, but renders it ephemeral up to the purest groan, an uncertain or ridiculous sign ('I am . . . hungry'), an ambiguous non-sign. The Stirnerian first person thus attains the *cogito* as a 'certitude évanouissante' (vanishing certainty) (Bréhier) or better yet as a 'pensée sans pensées' (thought without thoughts) (Bachelard). He knows that 'You are not thoughtless and speechless merely in (say) sleep, but even in the deepest reflection; yes, precisely

31 Stirner, *Ego and Its Own*, p. 245.

32 Stirner, *Ego and Its Own*, p. 220.

then most so'.[33] Simone Weil will go on to say one day that to rid oneself of a thought once and for all is the gate to eternity. 'The thought is my *own*', Stirner writes, 'only when I have no misgiving about bringing it in danger of death every moment, when I do not have to fear its loss as a *loss for me*, a loss of me'.[34] The absence of thought and speech is already in my every thought and word, and on this nothingness, on this pure having without being, Stirner based his cause: 'Feuerbach wants to smite Hegel's "absolute thinking" with *unconquered being*. But in me being is as much conquered as thinking is. It is *my* being, as the other is *my* thinking.'[35] The coincidence of having with the mere power of having, which zeroes out the being of having (the 'having' as being, as the being of a person, to be respected), which exposes this thought-being to nothingness without having anything to lose, can appropriate both thought and being. It is here that the simple statement of personal identity truly overcomes itself in the concept of unicity: 'If I were not this one, for instance, Hegel, I should not look at the world as I do look at it, I should not pick out of it that philosophical system which just I as Hegel do, etc'.[36] What is unique is not the 'je suis', which exempts one from adding 'Descartes', but every time the punctual coincidence of having, which zeroes out the being of a person and of thought in pure property, rendering every property unique (*that* world) and every person a singular, inimitable power and *that power* singularly personal, thus not belonging to everyone or to no one, not to one or to two, but to Hegel or otherwise to Descartes or to the same Stirner. On the stage of pure having every person has a power, every power of having has its own mask. And what thereby imposes itself is a comparison with the Aristotelian theory and paradox of the *habitus* (it is impossible to have a *habitus*, because it would produce the infinite regression of a having of

33 Stirner, *Ego and Its Own*, p. 306.

34 Stirner, *Ego and Its Own*, p. 302.

35 Stirner, *Ego and Its Own*, p. 300.

36 Stirner, *Ego and Its Own*, p. 301.

a having). What is at stake in Hegel's unicity is not in fact the habituality or the coherence of the temporal flow of an ego, a sequence of thought or (in Husserlian terms) of the 'stable properties' and therefore a style of change that constitutes the empirical, personal 'I' with its equally stable and permanent character. What we have is not therefore an 'inflection of being in having caused by a sort of inertia of duration',[37] but—despite the evidence—a having of being itself according to the unique singularity of a power. If in Hegel's system one therefore recognizes not so much the continuity of a substantial subject and of the related process of thought (of a systematic nature), not the flow that is identical to itself, but above all the historically unique intensity of a *Gewalt*, the unique breadth of a power, the resonance of an appropriation that by capturing consciousness itself extends itself over the world and, in grasping it, cancels out its being and reduces it to itself, that is to say to a pure having without substance.

. . . In the meantime, psychology turns political: if the cases of Meyer or Félida and Léonie forcefully emerge, attracting attention and requesting the control and articulation of a new science—from Frank to Pierre Janet—it is because they situate themselves in conformity with the efficient structure of the subject, which they both hide and allow one to glimpse in the form of excess and delirium, confining to the pathological the ambiguous mystery of individual personality. If compos sui *must be guaranteed and protected thus it is because the shift from pure intuition to substantial being occurred under the aegis of property and to the benefit of the proprietor. The internal struggle was closely related to social antagonisms and the effort that constituted personal identity was a war for the conservation of privileges, a defence or dissimulated theft from the vestments of the law. In this effort, having transforms into being, the psychological condition rises to the level of the State, and in it finds a new form, and the subject 'individualizes*

37 Paul Ricoeur, *À l'école de la phénoménologie* (Paris: Vrin, 2004[1986]), p. 120.

itself ever more perfectly' under the threat of death, fearing material loss and corporeal afflictions. A destructive tonality distinguishes the voice of the I that affirms itself only to reveal itself as a mine, *as that of a proprietor that does nothing but have, and who coincides entirely with his having and therefore with a 'having' that 'is' not something but subsists in the very absence of an object. It is precisely in the 'simple affirmation of personal identity' that naked possession appears, which is also the paradoxical and unalienable possession of privation, of cold, hunger, pain . . . Precisely that which in the sense of property-being constitutes loss, sacrifice and torment (and therefore provokes Marx's irony) now shows, as Tarde says, that 'l'être n'est pas tout le contenu de l'idée de propriété' (being is not the entire content of the idea of property), and therefore what one truly has is only the power of having and not the right to something, while being, as we know it, is nothing but a limitation of having. Even personal identity—a figure both obvious and confusing, abounding in metaphysical subtleties and theological niceties—once again finds its own conditions here . . .*

VI

Panorama

29. If the 'je est un autre' (I is another) is still a *je*, at least the *je* is not a *moi*. Doubleness thus reaffirms itself and spreads. Well before Pierre Janet's studies saw the light of day, before Marceline became famous, Félida X began to multiply, and in the most precipitous of ways, that is to say retrospectively. Reading in the pages of the *Revue scientifique* Azam's report to the Académie des sciences morales, Jean Charles François Dufay immediately felt like he recognized the singular behaviour of an old patient of his.

R. L., the patient that Dufay had kept under observation in 1845, was a 28-year-old seamstress, and a somnambulist since her earliest years. Her symptoms were quotidian and usually afflicted her at sundown or, if they were triggered by an excess of emotions, sometimes also in the morning, when the young woman collapsed all of a sudden, violently hitting her forehead on her work table, without however experiencing any pain. For her, the impact was in fact the entrance into her second life: she would get back up, and resume her duties at a good pace, as if nothing had happened, and indeed without even the need for the glasses which usually corrected her strong short-sightedness. She would then work for a long time and quite well, at that. And if she needed another bit of fabric, or perhaps a bow or a ribbon? Despite its being already dark, she had no need for a lamp to go down into her storehouse: she moved with assurance through the darkness, knowing where to find what she needed, in which cabinet and in which drawer. If perchance something was missing, she would replace it with whatever was at hand. Everything was easy for her: never a hesitation or a mistake or an accident. Thus, she continued, meticulous and dreaming, and she would end the day by leaving with her colleagues before going home to tranquilly rest. The next day she would be very surprised upon seeing that the work she had just begun was already finished.

Moreover, someone who had not been present at the beginning of the episode would not have noticed anything strange in R. L. Nothing, except for one detail: in the new phase, as Dufay writes, 'elle parle *nègre*' (she speaks black), replacing, as children do, the *je* with the *moi* and using verbs in the third person to distinguish her from herself: '"quand *moi* est bête" means when I am not somnambulating'.

The use of the *moi* thereby becomes the clear giveaway of the *dédoublement de la personnalité*. So it is for Dufay, and Azam agrees with his colleague, also recognizing the analogy with the case of Félida:

> It is an indisputable fact: Mademoiselle R. L. has two personalities. Although she is still Mademoiselle R. L., she not only possesses two distinct modes of being for someone observing her, but also for herself; indeed, she speaks of the *other* in the third person and in her first state she ignores everything she does in the second.[1]

But the solution certainly is not definitive, and Lignac's objection can be heard, even before Tarde, in the words of Egger: '*I* feel myself another, *I* am completely changed, *I* no longer recognize myself, *I* feel two men in *me*, *I* forget myself, *I* re-find myself'.[2] All of these expressions, he notes, make one think that the patients are conscious not only of an abnormal plurality but also of a fundamental psychic unity which they express by referring with the word 'I' to their entire existence. As James affirmed, commenting on Taine and especially Krishaber, in such cases, 'it is as

1 Azam, *Hypnotisme, double conscience et altérations de la personnalité*, p. 190.

2 Victor Egger, 'Analyse de l'ouvrage d'Azam' in Azam, *Hypnotisme, double conscience et altérations de la personnalité*, p. *xxxvii*.

certain that the *I* is unaltered as the *Me* is changed'. But this is precisely the first symptom of the illness, for the doctor or for the patient, and it is here that the difficulties and diatribes of the interpreters begin. Dufay's case does not escape this law, although the *moi* ('Moi bête, la fille bête' [Me stupid, the stupid girl]) is attributed to normal life by the one saying *je* and 'l'autre' is the primary personality for the secondary one that is conscious of it and speaks of it in its quaint jargon. For his part, Egger finds the most apt explanation: by using the *je* and the *moi* in such a way, R. L. is clearly aware that she is using two synonyms, and so precisely that which appears to be a sign of doubleness is in fact an ingenious stratagem used by the patient to say that she is always the same. As the philosopher writes in 1877, R. L. understands herself to be the one 'who changes the *quality*, the *manner of being*' without '*changing beings*, changing *personality*',[3] to then specify, ten years later, that 'distinguishing thus between two personalities, she affirms the unity of her person'.[4] The terms may vary, the psychological concept of personality, as we have seen with Azam, is not well-defined yet, but Egger insists on his opinion: the young seamstress cannot but be aware of a synonymy that—paradoxically—certifies personal identity. Thus, if a patient 'counts his *I*s (*moi*) [. . .] it is because he only has one of them';[5] and if a *je* says 'quand *moi* est bête' (when me is stupid), one must know how to recognize what is omitted and what is implied: 'quand *moi* est bête, il dit *je*' (when me is stupid, it says I). A truly double person would instead believe herself to be single in every phase of her life, completely unaware of the other 'I'—or indeed the doubling itself, which can be ascertained from an intersubjective point of view. Hence the strict conclusion: 'The terms of *double conscience* and of *dédoublement de la personnalité* have been employed with excessive carelessness'.[6]

---

3 Victor Egger and Léon Lereboullet, 'Étude psychologique et physiologique de l'amnésie dans certaines névroses' in Azam, *Hypnotisme, double conscience et altérations de la personnalité*, p. *xxv*.

4 Egger, 'Analyse de l'ouvrage d'Azam', p. *xxxvii*.

5 Egger, 'Analyse de l'ouvrage d'Azam', p. *xxxvii*.

6 Egger, 'Analyse de l'ouvrage d'Azam', p. *xxxvii*.

We might ask ourselves, on this topic, if the phrase 'unité de la personne' (unity of the person) has not been used with equally excessive carelessness, and if she who truly ignores the two *moi* believing herself to be one is the one who intentionally makes recourse to synonymy, relying on an expedient both too clever and too naive. In that case the friends and parents that recognize R. L.'s double life from the fact that all of a sudden 'elle parle *nègre*' would see her as double precisely because she considers herself one, in a reflection of her self-deception, and the true doubleness would be the one capable of escaping unnoticed even by an experienced observer such as Egger. The problem thus never ceases to generate new paradoxes.

30. 'An animal,' Maine de Biran writes in his *Mémoire sur la décomposition de la pensée*,

> can remain asleep even while various organs keep vigil; or it can awaken while thought and the 'I' are still asleep. It would not be impossible to observe these gradations or, perhaps, by tracing them back to their organic causes, to explain in this sense some effects of somnambulism.[7]

Egger's position is different: after having examined Azam's and Dufay's observations, he concludes that memory ties the somnambular 'I' to the normal one, the second personality to the first, and finally declares that 'the *dualité du moi*, mistakenly invented by the philosopher Maine de Biran to explain somnambulism, does not exist in either case.'[8] This attack on the *homo duplex* comes from a position (a theory of memory) that can be defined—in its own way and within certain limits—as Leibnizian:

> The 'I', according to this thesis, is not [. . .] in the effort; the present moment, in its special and new aspect, does not contain the elements of what the little words *je* and *moi*, if understood

7 Maine de Biran, *Mémoire sur la décomposition de la pensée*, p. 94.

8 Egger and Lereboullet, 'Étude psychologique et physiologique', p. *xxv*.

> correctly, signify. The 'I' is the total recollection, it is consciousness of the past as such, the series of past states of consciousness retained in the gaze of the present state and therefore summed up, condensed, through processes of a very mysterious nature whose results, however, are evident enough to constitute a factual truth.[9]

Writing these words in 1896, Egger too is re-reading and commenting on Leibniz:[10] but his is not a new interpretation of force as substance; rather, it is a revisitation of the theory of 'perceptions insensibles' (imperceptible perceptions) expostulated in the 'Preface' to the *Nouveaux essais sur l'entendement humain*.

As is well-known, for Leibniz these *petites perceptions* form and define the individual "I": their 'insensible variations' keep two beings from being identical by providing them with a difference 'plus que numérique' (more than numeric). We may recall the famous passage from the preface to the *Nouveau essais sur l'entendement humain*:

> These insensible perceptions also indicate and constitute the same individual, who is characterized by the vestiges or expressions which the perceptions preserve from the individual's former states, thereby connecting these with his present state. Even when the individual himself has no sense of the previous states, i.e. no longer has any explicit memory [*souvenir exprès*] of them, they could be known by a superior mind.[11]

Let us return to Egger's comment: permanent individuality is formed by the tenuous memory (*souvenir faible*) of the whole series of past states; although weak, such memory is always present and, as such, is tied to the state most clearly present (*fort présent*). The latter can also be, in its

9 Victor Egger, 'Le moi des mourants. Nouveaux faits', *Revue Philosophique de la France et de l'Étranger* 42 (1896): 339.

10 Egger, 'Le moi des mourants. Nouveaux faits': 339n1.

11 Gottfried Wilhelm Leibniz, *New Essays on Human Understanding* (Peter Remnant and Jonathan Bennett eds and trans) (Cambridge: Cambridge University Press, 1996), p. 55.

entirety or partially, constituted by an element of total recall that momentarily appears in its full light and is perceived in relation to the obscure *milieu* from which it has freed itself: this is, properly speaking, explicit memory.

The phrase *souvenir faible* is thus introduced and maintained within a double, coherent conceptual opposition: on the one hand, with respect to Leibniz's '*souvenir* exprès' and, on the other, to Egger's '*fort* présent'. The second oppositional relation (weak/strong) introduces the bond between *souvenir* and *présent*, and thereby between permanent identity, the totality of its traces, and the present, with which explicit memory must finally coincide. What is weak or strong in this schema, is the adherence of memories to the current present of the subject who says *je*—an adherence that can slacken (but not be interrupted) until it makes the personality and secondary modes of being appear, thus rendering necessary the *escamotage* of the synonym *moi*. The vigilant custodian of this connection is a particular *esprit supérieur*, the privileged observer capable of recognizing and explaining to others the synonymy, that is, to truly understand her who, to make herself be heard, comes to *parler nègre*.

Now, in Leibniz the insensible perceptions could not be called 'weak' or 'strong' in the same sense, because as such they are always clear, without any loss, to the supreme being. The *petites perceptions* maintain the strictest of autonomies from the present recollection of the individual, who depends on them. They remain insensible in ordinary sleep as they also do in that sleep or sudden metamorphosis of the monad that is commonly called death. To offer his partial interpretation of the Leibnizian passage, Egger must therefore separate it from the following equally well-known one: 'But those perceptions also provide the means for recovering this memory at need [. . .] That is why death can only be a sleep [. . .] in animals they are reduced to a state of confusion which puts awareness into abeyance but which cannot last for ever'.[12] This is clearly the argument of pre-established harmony, which must intervene

12 Leibniz, *New Essays on Human Understanding*, p. 55.

precisely here, but which instead disappears in Egger just as it does in Biran. Yet again, the Leibnizian model of individuality is thus deprived of its essential content; and just as Biran's time was the time of consciousness and the force was the force of the 'I', so for Egger the unity of the person belongs to the subject that says *je* or *moi*.

Once more, the definition of the pathology confirms the bond between individual life and consciousness, relegating the absence of apperceptions to death. And if the matter of the 'I' is not immobile or 'fuyante comme le fait présent' (fleeting like the present) but 'progressive', then the I does not form by following the development of this ever-richer matter, but in the 'reflection that condenses and organizes'. A possible completion is thus posited, in which the subject coincides with itself once and for all or, in other words, a consciousness or a memory of individuality in its entirety. A present is posited beyond which there is no present, a limit of duration in which every latency becomes explicit and the whole *moi* (every *souvenir*) clings to the *je*. The result is that culmination and distinctive sensation of individuality that Egger calls the *moi vif*, an expression that recalls Leibniz's *vis viva* but which also inscribes the affirmation of the 'I' in the negative halo of death. And if he who sees death sees life, it is because without the memory of the latter the former would merely be an empty frame. On the other hand, life remains just an evanescent image if it is not grasped in its completeness from the definitive point of view, in the final hour, or rather at every moment, under the constant threat of death: only the latter traces all of the latent memories back to the current personality.

The *fait primitif* of *effort* and of *résistance* is thus replaced by Egger with 'the evidence of a factual truth': at the moment of death, the subject sees and appropriates himself 'with a type of reaction', as if his memories ended up crowding together at their limit and gathered as a counter-reaction in a vision that contains them all, being the last, unmemorable and unforgettable one. The *moi vif*, the true individual 'I' is thus, according to Egger's most famous title, *Le moi dei mourants*, and a paradoxical illumination of the shadows reunites every 'souvenir faible et toujours présent' with the 'fort présent', recalling it *in extremis* with expressive formulas, but also summing it up in a succession of images or in the single visual of a panorama. Words can indeed be meditated on at length, and require in any case the methodical slowness of reasoning, whereas a series of images passes quickly, as in a dream, in the face of an imminent end.

While the now-cinematographic rapidity thus mimics the instantaneous brevity of intuition, and Cartesian lucidity is converted into an oneiric projection, individuality and the reflecting consciousness find themselves rigorously united at the extreme limit.

This certainly was not the case for Leibniz. As Egger himself is forced to admit, in the 'Preface' to the *Nouveaux essais* individuality is not defined using the term *moi*, which possesses instead 'un sens métaphysique' (a metaphysical meaning).[13] As one reads in §30 of the *Monadologia*, reflexive acts make us think of 'ce qui s'appelle Moy et [. . .] considérer que ceci ou cela est en nous' (what is called the self, and consider that this or that is within us). But to think one's own 'I' means thinking Being and Substance together, the simple and the composite, the immaterial and God Himself, the finite and the infinite. Thus, reflection does not limit itself to personality, while the latter does not limit itself to consciousness. And if for no being is sleep eternal, in rational ones it does not last at all, since they are 'destined to retain the personhood that was given them in the city of God'. Here, pre-established harmony reigns. And it is only when the latter is dethroned—with an act of conscious substitution—that consciousness coincides with individual personality, every memory belongs to the *moi*, and every act or judgement is attracted into and confined within the frame of death. That void which is in every thought, and 'even in the deepest concentration of thought', is now filled by the 'I' or by 'personality'—but at the ultimate price.

13 Egger, 'Le moi des mourants. Nouveaux faits': 339n1.

31. 'The topic of the panoramic vision of the dying has occupied Bergson for a while . . .'[14] Thus begins the essay by Georges Poulet dedicated to the passages that, from *Matière et mémoire* to the lectures of *Énergie spirituelle*, between 1896 to 1913, mark the stages of a meditation developed, among apparent uncertainties and rethinkings, until its clearest expression at the Oxford conference of 1911 on the *Perception du changement*. In *Matière et mémoire*, Bergson harkens back to the now-canonical studies authored by Alfred Maury (*Le sommeil et les rêves*, 1861–65), Ribot (*Les maladies de la mémoire*, 1881) and cites Forbes Winslow who, in *Obscure Diseases of the Brain and Mind* (1860), had examined the prodigious memory of individuals suffering from asphyxiation, capable of reliving their entire past in a series of extraordinarily clear images. From the very beginning, the privileged source is in any case Egger's article on the *Moi des mourants*, from which the philosopher of *durée* extracts, arguments, testimonials and, in part, inspiration: perhaps nothing could in fact be more striking for him than 'this Leibnizian affirmation of total recall and of its identification with consciousness'.[15] Stimulated by these readings, Bergson would go on to completely reinvent the problem, tying in an original way the apparition of the *souvenir total* not to a hyperactivity of the soul but, against his predecessors, to the relaxation of a habitual tension. As Poulet also notes, Egger's *moi vif* corresponded to a state of attention antithetical to any *détente*, to a vivacity of sentiment that cannot be interpreted if not as 'an extreme concentration of one's forces, as a petrification in the face of peril'.[16]

In reality, one must add that Egger does not entirely overlook the phenomenon of beatitude or better yet the dying individual's *bien-être* (which is accounted for in the first of his examples, that of the mountain climber who falls), all while insisting—as he will once again in the

14 Georges Poulet, 'Bergson: Le thème de la vision panoramique des mourants et la juxtaposition' in *L'espace proustien* (Paris: Gallimard, 1982[1963]), p. 167.

15 Poulet, 'Bergson', p. 178.

16 Poulet, 'Bergson', p. 175.

answer to Paul Sollier's objection—on the *suractivité* of memory and intelligence. Compared with the positivity of the latter, and precisely in the quick succession of images from the past, the singular, relaxed tranquillity of the falling climber can be explained by the suppression of sensibility whose complement is a condition of no less remarkable happiness. If for Aristotle pleasure is the epiphenomenon of the act, 'le bien-être, la "douceur" est ici l'épiphénomène du moins-être et du non-acte' (the well-being, the sweetness is here the epiphenomenon of diminished being or of non-action).[17] It is precisely this gentle relaxing of sensations (or of resistance), this paradoxical sense of indifference, that is filled with a host of memories: anaesthesia generate hypermnesia, or in other words the *moi vif*, which reveals itself to be, in contrast with what Poulet argued, entirely coherent with *détente*.

It is well known that for Bergson our habitual behaviour, entirely directed towards action, cannot but overlook pure memory. Dedicated to the transformation of the present into the future, we make use of the past by selecting it, far from renouncing it we use it and thus we overlook and loose it. It is not so, however, for the moribund: in his last moments without activity, relieved, one might say, of the future's compulsion, he enjoys the restitution of lost time. 'The scenes of his early life', Winslow wrote, relaying the testimony of a man who had accidentally survived a suicide attempt, 'were in their minutest particulars revived [. . .] The remembrance of faces [. . .] was restored to his recollection [. . .] every trifling and minute circumstance connected with his past life was presented to his mind like so many charming pictorial sketches and paintings'.[18]

For his part, Poulet opportunely cites the letter that Bergson wrote to James on 25 March 1903, recalling the most famous image from *Matière et mémoire*: '"the unity of the I" that philosophers speak of seems

17 Egger, 'Le moi des mourants. Nouveaux faits': 347.

18 Forbes Winslow, *Obscure Diseases of the Brain and Mind* (Philadelphia: Lea, 1866[1860]), p. 285.

to me like the union of a culmination or summit in which I withdraw with an effort of attention, an effort that prolongs itself throughout all of life and which, as it seems to me, is the essence of my life'.[19] To return from this summit to the base, to the state in which one finds all of the moments of the past disseminated, Bergson continues, one would have to relax one's concentration and enter into a dispersive state, one of dreaming; not give oneself things to do but rather to undo, and to lose more than to acquire or gain. My memories are in fact already present, even if I do not perceive them, and when they return to consciousness 'nothing truly new is produced'.

Of course, in these lines, it is all of Bergsonism that is at play in the comparison with Leibniz and also with Maine de Biran. We recognize the fundamental terms: during its moment of glory (one may think precisely of James), the concept of *effort* takes on a typical inflection starting from the *Essai sur les données immédiates de la conscience* and attains that philosophical clarity that Albert Thibaudet opposed to the willed obscurity of Ernest Renan's *nisus*[20] in the lecture on *Effort intellectuel* (1902), to later extend its dominion to the quasi-metaphorical breadth which from the *Évolution créatrice*, and finally to the moral and social sphere of the *Deux sources* as an 'effort sur soi-même' (the state of tension or contraction in which, resisting against our resistances, we obey a duty or respect an obligation). In 1896, *effort* was a synonym of attention for Bergson, or rather it designated the double undertaking, the 'double effort' by which the past, i.e. memory, compels perception ('to insert the largest possible part of itself into the present action')[21] while perception orients memory, selects the past and appropriates it. The upturned cone from *Matière et mémoire* is traversed and formed by the attention that finally concentrates the 'I' in the point of present perception and of contact with reality. And one might observe that what is at stake in the

19 Poulet, 'Bergson', p. 196.

20 Albert Thibaudet, *Trente ans de vie* française, Le Bergsonisme, VOL. 3 (Paris: Gallimard, 1924[1923]), p. 150.

21 Bergson, *Matter and Memory*, p. 168.

effort is the question of habit, that the somatic traits symbolize 'l'effort accumulé des actions passées' (the accumulated effect of past actions) in man—just as one might otherwise think of the *effort* of intuition, which attains novelty and liberates comprehension from all false, habitual platitudes . . . And of course we will remember the apex (*point*) of the famous cone while reading in the *Évolution créatrice* that 'the brain is the sharp edge (*pointe*) with which consciousness cuts into the compact tissue of events'.[22] What is at play, in the phenomenon of panoramic vision as well, is nothing less than the cerebral organ or the Bergsonian theory of the body, the relation of 'solidarité' between the body and consciousness, the (disjunctive) intersection of matter and life, necessity, automatism and creation.

In his lectures on *Matière et mémoire*, Merleau-Ponty speaks of an unresolved 'va-et-vient' between the point and the base of the cone, polemically observing that Bergson is unable to articulate the two planes and describes them while he tries in vain to bring them into a synthesis by assembling two objective elements, 'le percept pur et le souvenir pur' (pure perception and pure recollection).[23] Vladimir Jankélévitch had already observed, however, that 'harmony is always born in moments of crisis, that is to say, of the greatest distinction'.[24] Now, it is precisely the *effort* that maintains the solidarity not only of the body with the spirit but also of the base of the cone with the point, of memory of the past with perception. Thus the *détente* is not just a pause or a correlate of the effort but a relaxation of the solidarity that ties consciousness to the body. If there is an *effort*, if there is a *détente*, if the Bergsonian *effort* is not, like that of Biran, tied to the resistance of the body but '*tendu vers la détente*',[25] it is because the spirit (or 'le moi') outdoes the body, remaining irreducible to its material and spatial imprisonment. Panoramic

22 Henri Bergson, *Creative Evolution* (Arthur Mitchell trans.) (Mineola, NY: Dover Publications, Inc., 1998), p. 263.

23 Merleau-Ponty, *Incarnate Subject*, p. 91.

24 Jankélévitch, *Henri Bergson*, p. 85.

25 Jankélévitch, *Bergson*, p. 115.

vision is then the slackening or the development of all images or in other words the relaxation of all efforts, not the giving in of a last resistance but the loosening of *effort* as such in the solution or the dissolution of corporeal constriction.

32. To Egger's alpinist, total recall appeared under the sign of 'moins-être' or of a 'non-acte'. And if hypermnesic vitality compensated for inaction, this was, in turn, a side-effect of the anaesthesia. For Bergson, however, 'to lose', 'to undo' are the highest of philosophical operations, aimed at the attainment of true relaxation, in which alone, 'the image of our past in general', 'studied at length, or rather examined with a mental microscope' could restore 'in the smallest of details our anterior life'.[26]

Now, this vision cannot be reduced to solitude or to reflexive inactivity. Philosophy, as Bachelard would later say, does not see to 'organize inaction'. It is not a spiritualist balsam, not a shelter or a comfort from mundane travails, it is not a pause in Grateloup, with its uncertain satisfactions. Already in a page from his youth, Bergson had written that 'the thought of Maine de Biran was voluntarily withdrawing into itself; it turned towards the inside, taut in an effort of internal vision',[27] recognizing instead the model for a new Biranism—both faithful and, in its active temperament, emancipated—in the philosophy of Paul Janet: indeed, when Janet interrogates consciousness it is not out of a sort of self-satisfaction but because for him philosophy is a 'speculation that extends into action'. Insisting on the same model, the older Bergson, as is well known, will instead go on to establish his own distance from the doctrines of spiritualism: 'Certainly they are right to listen to conscience [. . .] but the intellect is there [. . .] They are right to believe in the absolute reality of the person [. . .] but . . . '.[28] Punctuating the end of the

26 Henri Bergson, 'Le problème de la personnalité' in *Écrits philosophiques*, p. 429.

27 Henri Bergson, 'Compte rendu des Principes de métaphysique et de psychologie de Paul Janet' in *Écrits philosophiques*, p. 212.

28 Bergson, *Creative Evolution*, p. 268.

third chapter of *Évolution créatrice*, this series of but's does not of course aim at converting thought into action by overcoming both Biran's withdrawal and Janet's exemplary longing: if it can 'introduce us into spiritual life' in a sense that would differ from that of spiritualism, it is not by extending into activity but because it can comprise together action, intelligence, and the matter of the disinterested sphere of intuition. As an immediate knowledge 'of the spirit by the spirit', the latter does not isolate use from the living or material world but reaches the matter and life that are in us. Remaining obscure to intelligence, it understands intelligence itself; it consists in an effort of internal vision, yes, but one that is anything but closed off within itself: 'Let us then go down', to use the words of the famous 1911 conference in Bologna, *L'intuition philosophique*, 'into our inner selves: the deeper the point we touch, the stronger the stronger will be the thrust that send us back to the surface. Philosophical intuition is this contact, philosophy is this impetus [élan]'.[29] And if the intuitions end up being too vague, still discontinuous, tiresome and incomplete, philosophy will have to take possession of them, 'first to sustain them, and then to broaden and connect them amongst each other.'

With its *élan* beyond corporeal resistance, intuitive effort does not therefore lead to action or inaction but rather—to quote another famous phrase—consists in the inversion of the usual, analytical operation of intelligence, it is the exit from the social bond or somnambulism that inaugurates a new paradigm of self-consciousness: 'there is one reality, at least, which we all seize from within, by intuition and not by simple analysis. It is our own personality in its flowing through time—our self which endure. We may sympathize intellectually with nothing else, but we certainly sympathize with ourselves'.[30]

29 Henri Bergson, 'Philosophical Intuition' in *Henri Bergson: Key Writings* (Keath Ansell Pearson and John Mullarkey eds) (New York, NY: Continuum, 2002), p. 244.

30 Bergson, *Introduction to Metaphysics*, p. 7.

There is a decisive theoretical correspondence, aside from a chronological proximity, between these words from the *Introduction à la métaphysique* (1903) and those, already cited, addressed to James: the distinction that Bergson makes here between *analyse* and *intuition* can easily be mapped onto the one where, in the letter, he opposes the normal condition of *concentration* to the oneiric state of *dispersion*. Dream and intuition can now reveal their affinity and, combined in philosophical vision, become less uncertain: *perdre* and *défaire* appear as the highest inclination of thought, coherent with the intuitive *effort* and with the panoramic vision that supports, expands, and connects even the vaguest of images or the most ephemeral of illuminations.

33. Poulet's study reconstructs the history of a lengthy theoretical anguish and the image of an undecided philosopher, torn between the principles of activity (or of the will) and *détente*; a philosopher who finally had to conceptualize—precisely in the *Introduction à la metaphysique*—his theory of the 'conversion de l'attention' to apply it with exactitude to the subject of panoramic vision and to reach a clear position, devoid of complications ('Philosopher est un acte simple' [Philosophizing is a simple act]) or ambiguities. Only a renewed conception of attention—which in order to be real like *durée* had to be distracted from the goals of everyday activity—could in fact reveal itself to be worthy of *détente*.

This is what occurs in 1911, at the Oxford lectures on the *Perception du changement*. The habitual distinction between the present and the past—Bergson now explains—is relative and even arbitrary. It is relative to the state of attention, for which the 'present' is that which corresponds to its effort, and that which does not fall under its interest will *ipso fact* be past; and it is nevertheless arbitrary, since *durée* is not subject to any practical circumstances. Hence a sufficiently powerful attention to life, one capable of advancing beyond the limits imposed by action, would embrace in a single *présent indivisé* the entire past of the conscious person, not as a collection of simultaneous parts but as the continuous and continuously mobile presence, whose perpetuity will have nothing immutable about it and whose indivisibility will not have an instantaneous nature, in other words, as 'un présent qui dure' (a present that lasts).[31]

Philosophy, or true metaphysics, thus coincides with a new *epistrophé*, understood as the education of attention, the habit of not separating the present from the past that it carries with it. And thanks to this capacity to sustain and prolong intuition, everything begins to move, 'everything comes to life around us, everything is revivified in us. A great impulse carries beings and things along . . . '.[32]

But if this philosophy can be something other than a flight towards the Empyrean or towards Grateloup and therefore comparable—as will be confirmed by Jankélévitch's Plotinian *Henri Bergson* or Bréhier's Bergsonian *Plotin*—to the intimate contemplation of the *Enneads*, it is because its 'conversion' is not presumed or imaginary. If attention to the present seems limited and weakened, it is by virtue of a more powerful attention that serves as a counterbalance. And thus, the evidence of the past's conservation or of pure memory responds to the vagueness of the pre-philosophical intuition: 'That is not a hypothesis. It happens in exceptional cases that the attention suddenly loses the interest it had in life: immediately, as though by magic, the past once more becomes present'.[33] Precisely in those who are exposed to the danger of death, for the mountain climber who falls, for one who risks drowning or is about to be hanged (these are the examples taken from Egger), there is a 'sudden conversion of attention' or in other words a new orientation of consciousness, which will no longer be 'turned to the future and absorbed by the necessities of action'. And 'that is enough', as Bergson adds, 'to call to mind a thousand different "forgotten" details and to unroll the whole history of the person before him in a moving panorama [*mouvant panorama*]'.[34]

---

31 Henri Bergson, 'The Perception of Change' in *Henri Bergson*: *Key Writings*, p. 262.

32 Bergson, 'Perception of Change', p. 266.

33 Bergson, 'Perception of Change', p. 262.

'*That* is enough': the spectre of death, which by projecting itself onto life inverts the sense of action, revealing thus its recondite presence and its paradigmatic and essential function as the pivot-point of the entire Bergsonian construction. The example of the last mnesic panorama, whether it be Egger's or Winslow's, is much more than merely an example amongst others where the possibility of philosophical life remains tied to the end of the concerned life: it is in fact simply death, as the crude negation of the future, that rids us of all of our anxieties. In the face of that first intuition, the current of the future, that is of life, of intelligence, of interest, opens up; in the face of that current the barrier of death now rears itself, which, insuperable by the interested aptitude, forces the present and duration, the present and the movement to reveal their coincidence, actuating the *epistrophé* of attention.

Only on this basis, as Bergson later writes, 'does memory not necessitate explanations' (nothing in fact now separates it from intelligence) and the first intuition consolidates itself, in the fullest becoming of philosophy. Only in this transition, in this brutal inversion, does the metaphysical gaze disclose itself, and the *grand élan* can grab us and carry us away with it. Egger's *moi vif* does not then seem to be very far away, when attention and *détente* no longer contradict each other. And like this new idea of attention and the last aura that the falling alpinist or the hanged man enjoys, this vital élan and the fall into the void also reveal an unexpected affinity.

34. With the coinage offered by Egger, Bergson can now once again lend shape to the classic formula of duration or of the 'melody which one perceives as indivisible'.[35] Indeed, already in the *Essai sur les données immédiates de la conscience*, the 'durée toute pure' (pure duration) as a 'form that assumes the succession of our states of consciousness when our I *lets itself live*',[36] when every order and succession gives way, when

34 Bergson, 'Perception of Change', p. 263.

35 Bergson, 'Perception of Change', p. 262.

36 Henri Bergson, *Essai sur les données immédiates de la conscience* (Paris: Presses Universitaires de France, 1948[1889]), pp. 74–75; emphasis mine.

space ceases to intrude on time and the antinomies of continuity and discontinuity, of the one and the many dissolve. Then, 'remembering these states [the I] does not juxtapose them with the current one as one point can be juxtaposed with another, but organizes them, as can happen when we remember the notes of a melody fused together, so to speak.'[37]

Panoramic movement or indivisible music, *durée pure* or *mémoire pure*, *détente* or philosophy . . . the names vary, follow and overlap in a spectrum of chromaticisms. 'A musician at heart,' Bergson 'loves musical analogies,' writes Jankélévitch, the interpreter most sensitive to this aspect, who observes that Bergsonism 'est le temps retrouvé' (is time regained): if it is not an effort directed at interiority (like that of Maine de Biran) or a reflection that extends into action (like that of Paul Janet), if it is a philosophy that, in discovering the continuity and indivisibility of interior life liberates itself from habit and all social representations, it is insofar as it draws on the mobile scene of the past.

Irreducible to the consequences of anaesthesia, for Bergson the disinterested vision of the alpinist is born of the 'threat of sudden death'[38] or in other words from the equally 'sudden conviction that the moment is the moment of death [*qu'on va mourir à l'instant*].'[39] Only this fatal instant offers in fact the privilege of panoramic totality. And precisely the fact of its being the last for the intelligence in question or, as Egger specified, the belief of its being thus, frees it from its nature, from its instantaneous solitude, conferring onto it the melodic tenor of duration. We will therefore have to define this privilege better to proceed along the way indicated by Poulet. We know that man for Bergson is the being that is not only conscious but capable—unlike animals—of liberating his consciousness from the slavery of the present, that is, 'of calling up the recollection at will [. . .] independently of the present perception'[40]

37 Bergson, *Essai sur les données immédiates de la conscience*, p. 75.

38 Bergson, 'Perception of Change', p. 262.

39 Henri Bergson, 'Phantasms of the Living and Psychical Research' in *Mind-Energy*, p. 95.

40 Bergson, *Creative Evolution*, p. 180; see Bergson, *Matter and Memory*, pp. 102–3.

and to dream. But we also know that the dream corresponds to loss, that when we abandon ourselves to the dream, ceasing to act, our 'I'—as one reads in the *Évolution créatrice*—'s'éparpille' (is scattered).[41] Thus, a human being capable of dreaming his own existence instead of living it—as is said in *Matière et mémoire*—would have an infinite multitude of details before his eyes, and the past—as *L'évolution créatrice* specifies[42]—would decompose for him 'is broken up into a thousand recollections made external to one another'.[43] The dreamer sees 'en raccourci' (in a nutshell), his memories crowd in his mind and fly past in a few moments, but without losing their differences: they gather while remaining separate and maintaining their obstinate individuality they cannot meld into a single melody. The dream, as we will see, is hence akin to the disorientation of vertigo: like the latter, it is a crisis of perception, and therefore of action and presence.

The dreaming 'I' is a ravished and dispersed 'I' and it will not find itself in yearning to die. The moribund, on the other hand, or else he who truly believes in an imminent end, does not dream with his eyes open; he cannot sleep, knowing that he will not wake up; he cannot separate himself from the present that he perceives as the last and of which he has never had such an acute sensation. A simple yielding of action or attention still has a way open before it; a dream might condense the images of an entire life into a few instants. But if these are evidently the last, if *they are already* all of life and all of time presses against the present, memory truly (that is, without effort) begins to move: no longer having to liberate a future, it is not forced to insert itself continuously into the moving habit, and the waking man no longer has to grant it to action and perception. Now relaxation rules, and no longer impedes attention, which can turn to the mobility of the panorama, being now removed from any finality, held back and at the same time transformed into a special instant that is the paradigm and the *raison d'être* of those

41 Bergson, *Creative Evolution*, p. 103.

42 Bergson, *Creative Evolution*, p. 103.

43 Bergson, *Creative Evolution*, p. 201.

rare moments of existence in which 'we attain ourselves'—not the last of a meagre series, but the first to which others refer, the moment, both definitive and exemplary, of their relative exceptionality. It is precisely for this reason, that is to say, only because our attention will one day in any case be suddenly turned away from everyday worries that we can have sporadic intuitions. And their rarity is not a merit but merely a sign of fragility: they are sporadic and brief because every time they are reconsigned to the past by the impulse of the future, because they cannot be definitive. Philosophy, on the other hand, prolongs and fortifies intuition, and provides an education, if one can say so, in view of the final panorama. To the illuminations that suspend habit only to then be immediately overcome by it, it opposes the motto of a new habit without interruptions: 'ne jamais isoler le présent du passé qu'il traîne avec lui' (never isolate the present from the past it carries with it).[44]

35. When the extreme situation is transformed into a philosophical predisposition, the threat dissipates, and death loses its power. Nevertheless, one might observe, that last instant retains its exemplary nature, and it is still such only if one believes it to be so, that is, for an interested consciousness. Precisely for that reason it captures one's attention and purifies it, rendering its very own philosophical conversion possible. For this reason, in other words, the truth of philosophy still depends on belief and interest. Bergsonism, one might add, owes too much to the testimonials cited by Egger: in order to become a simultaneously attentive and relaxed vision he had to admit, thus transforming it into a 'continuellement présent' (continually present), the reality of the threat that constitutes them as such—and *that* is enough. As a consequence, the 'se laisse vivre' (lets itself live) in the 'Essai'—an expression that recurs in 1902, next to 'relâchement' (relaxation)[45]—will be nothing more than a relaxation and a letting oneself live in the moment when one is to die. And if it does not consist in a deferment, in a supplementary duration

44 Bergson, 'Perception of Change', p. 265.

45 Bergson, *Mind-Energy*, p. 185.

granted to a time that is already *durée*, movement, melody, it is because it derives from that last vision, it is a panorama reduced to habit. If the 'conversion' that Bergson speaks of in 1911 thus finds a certain equivalent in the famous dictum of the *Introduction à la métaphysique* ('Philosopher consiste à invertir la direction habituelle du travail de la pensée' [Philosophizing consists in inverting the habitual direction of the work of thinking]); if the philosopher, able to *défaire* and *perdre*, exercises and maintains this new, slackened attention, that is irreducible to the processes of intelligence, and that is coherent with intuition as disinterested instinct (*L'évolution créatrice*), if the entire life of consciousness discloses itself for him and flows in every present and every past, it is because he lives in the most paradoxical of ways, not preparing himself for death, but enacting constantly the experience of the moribund. As if he could free us from the instantaneous constriction by rendering it continuous, Bergson—precisely he, the metaphysician who 'suppresses death'[46]—thus inscribed time and, even before Heidegger, philosophy itself into the insuperable horizon or the continuous imminence of the end. But this conclusion must at least be pondered: to truly think the experience of the dying means *ipso facto* liberating pure memory *in every present*, so that the new habit will be nothing other than its own movement, the flowing melody will not cease, just as it has never ceased to flow. Not only did the past or its memory lie in fact since forever at the base of the cone, or better yet, not only a still unforeseen thought, but the very conversion or possibility of the impetus: the testimonial of the dying man is this memory-thought, and philosophy itself was already there, at the deepest point, and for that very reason it does not teach us something, it does not induce us to anything, it merely educates one to oneself. It is attention, rather, that slackens and transforms when it sees itself in the testimony and meets its own limit. If therefore at least for once the living man will recognize himself in him who is about to drown, if he believes his report, prolonging his own interest in the paradoxical

---

46 Max Horkheimer, 'On Bergson's Metaphysics of Time' (Peter Thomas trans.), *Radical Philosophy* 131 (2005): 14.

relaxedness of the other, the 'ne jamais isoler' (never isolate) will not sound like an imperative and will not require an effort of the will. The present will no longer be isolated 'du passé qu'il traîne avec lui' (from the past it carries with it): made true and long-lasting by the gaze of the dying man, intuition will be able to reabsorb him into its own light. 'This is enough' to render any separation impossible.

... Inspired by psychological research, philosophy, which had transformed pure thought or intuition into effort—now that effort (or attention) was no longer the voluntary act of a single individual but, in the relation to matter, an undertaking now 'commune à tous' (common to all)—now had to raise itself on the basis it had just attained, in order to not lose itself. With an interpretation as brilliant as it was laden with ambiguity, the Leibnizian theory of memory had to be associated with individual identity and the vertiginous and 'confused perceptions'—which Egger calls 'faibles' (weak) and which Bergson reserves for the 'esprit imparfait' (imperfect spirit), attributing them to the perception of extension'[47]*—could join and save themselves in a 'panoramic vision of the past [. . .] due, then, to a sudden* disinterestedness in life, *born of the sudden conviction that the moment is the moment of death'.*[48] *Confirming the link between* effort *and threat, the absence of the former appeared as the privilege granted to one who is about to die, and in the meantime this individual became the true proprietor, that is, the inheritor of history and of duration itself. It is precisely the theory of* durée, *which places itself in opposition to the atomistic conception of temporality, that had to thus remain singularly tied to the gaze of the moribund, as the* détente *revealed its tacit, singular, inalienable relation to the last attention, or rather with the conversion* in articulo mortis, *and with the faith, equally typical of the individual in question, in the fatal instant ...*

47 Bergson, *Creative Evolution*, p. 351.

48 Bergson, 'Phantasms of the Living and Psychical Research', p. 95.

VII

No One's Dream

36. Personality, as Bergson affirms in 1914, is the problem of problems, the centre around which all philosophies gravitate or should gravitate.[1] In the meantime, the debate surrounding *dédoublement* dominates the pages of Ribot's *Revue philosophique*, where, as a result of a coherent development, it has now replaced the lengthy discussion surrounding suggestion and artificial somnambulism. Bergson, who in 1886 had analysed subjects under hypnosis and their unconscious simulations, now returns in the *Conférence de Madrid sur l'âme humaine* (1916) to the famous case of Bourne/Brown studied by James, reflects on Félida X's *amnésie périodique*, and draws up an original diagnosis. Harkening back, one might say, to Pierre Janet's detailed criticism (in addition to the studies on 'psychasthénie'), he overturns Azam's reconstruction and hierarchy: if there has ever been an 'abnormal' stage in Félida's double life, it is in fact precisely the one that Azam called the 'first one' and which he considered to be closer to the normal state of the young, closed-off asthenic. The pathological phase thus does not correspond to a second consciousness but to a suspension of memory or a somnambular state in which the young woman falls when 'she does not have sufficient strength to retain all of her memories': in Bergson's view, Félida is an adolescent who, suffering excessively from the challenges and troubles imposed by growth, becomes taciturn and shy, withdraws from the world, but thanks to these restful and compensatory pauses gradually

1 Bergson, 'Le problème de la personnalité', pp. 418–19.

recovers her strength, until her personality, which essentially is and has always been single, stabilizes. It is precisely the apparent *dédoublement* that confirms the primacy of the very individuality that it was meant to controvert and dethrone.

The first and the second state therefore unite as weariness and rest under the renewed sign of *effort*, that is, of a quotidian effort common to all that is usually unapparent, but which can nevertheless reveal itself in certain cases in all of its complexity. So it was for Azam's patient; so it is, less intensely, for every one of us: personality 'demands efforts [. . .] represents an exhausting effort. It is tiresome to be a person just as it is tiresome to remain standing or to walk on one's own two feet'.[2] But for Bergson, a reader of Ernst Haeckel, all of natural history is the story of a thousand-year-old effort accomplished by all beings and oriented towards an affirmation of human personality. The *effort* of the single individual thus participates in the enormous effort that no one can escape.

37. The *dédoublement*, which *Matière et mémoire* already explained as a mechanical diminution of the sensory-motor apparatus, harkens back, in fact, to the fundamental opposition between *durée* or life and the *étendue* of matter. An expression of the former that must apply to the latter, consciousness—as one reads in the *Évolution créatrice*—is *split*, divided between intelligence and intuition. Between the two of them, life and matter produce *effort*, and we know that for Bergson it is only where the current of one encounters the cliff of the other, only in these vortices, that invention and evolution are born. Here one also incidentally finds his criticism of Leibniz: the pre-established harmony, as the extreme outcome of finalist doctrine, is nothing but an inverted mechanism in which 'tout est donné' (everything is given), everything follows a program—and in the absence of anything unforeseen, there is no creation, and time itself becomes superfluous.

---

2 Henri Bergson, 'Conférence de Madrid sur l'âme humaine' in *Écrits philosophiques*, p. 521.

As if in a singular new version of the *homo duplex*, personality is therefore still maintained and shaped by effort: when the sensory-motor apparatus loses its vigour, attention dulls and the adaptation to the present situation (that is, the relation to matter) slackens, then the *dédoublement* occurs. But this duplication also indicates an excess: if personality splits, it is because as spirit and intuition it exists beyond intelligence, the brain and the senses—and if it exists beyond intelligence, it survives the body and every effort. It therefore defines itself precisely through and beyond matter, or in other words through and beyond organic death: in its spiritual essence it is actually *untied* from the body. If in Leibniz, or in pre-established harmony, the body is indestructible, the soul is immortal and the two remain bonded by the *vinculum substantiale*, in Bergson an already-outlined and vague individuality concretizes precisely in the encounter with matter: in whirlwinds and resistances, souls ceaselessly create and determine themselves, even though 'in a certain sense they already existed'. But this *préexistence*, being the pre-existence of something that survives, is perhaps in turn only a retrospective projection of *survivance*, and derives from the disconnect of the soul from the body or, in other words, from the disintegration of the latter. If in the *Monadologia* immortality is distinguished from indestructibility, and the indestructible resists death as the rapid variation of constitutive relations, in Bergson the soul or the person is 'immortal' also with respect to an organism that simply disintegrates and dies. What is therefore decisive, specifically for vitalist philosophy, is the limit of biological life: to meld once again with everything it must respect an unconfessed duty, it must declare between the lines that the return to that which has always pre-existed, the jump beyond individuation, is only made possible through individual corporeal death. It is in the shadow of the latter that the efforts of action and intelligence are joined by those typical of the philosopher, stretched beyond the limits of the body, of matter, space, and individuality itself, towards the immense and relaxed flow of life.

38. Thirty years before Maine de Biran interpreted it in light of *effort*, the bond between personality and property emerged as an epochal problem. Kant's theoretical rigour was matched by Johan Wolfgang von Goethe's historical sensibility. Thus, 'the rise of the word [. . .] was simultaneously its decline', with the most exemplary limitation to empirical character and individuality.[3] The *Critique of Practical Reason* responded to the need to free the person of possession and antagonisms, identifying it instead with moral law. In *Wilhelm Meisters Lehrjahre*, personality appeared on the contrary in its current identification with property, with the landed aristocracy. Only the aristocrat, the proprietor, could *be* a personality. The bourgeois, on the other hand, yearned for a personality that was ever denied him—as Goethe explains—except on stage, that is only, once again, as a mask. Once *again* as a mask, or in other words once more according to the well-known older meaning of 'person' that the individual put on in the theatre as in society; and *only* because on the social stage the person now coincided with aristocratic having and being, that the bourgeois could only feign and imitate, within the old unities of the canon, which were in turn temporally and spatially subordinated to the social rituality that regulates the opening of the proscenium. The idea of baroque metaphysics, according to which the 'spectateurs croient voir la même chose, et s'entre-entendent en effet, quoique chacun voie et parle selon la mesure de sa vue' (spectators think they see the same thing and are agreed about it, although each one sees or speaks according to the measure of his vision),[4] is now weighed on by the partition of political economy, which by dividing the theatre of the world into classes reunites and once again divides monads, broadens or constricts points of view within assigned limits. Thus, the paradigm of the puppets and then the role of the theatre company in Wilhelm's

3 Theodor W. Adorno, 'Gloss on Personality' in *Critical Models: Interventions and Catchwords* (Henry W. Pickford trans.) (New York, NY: Columbia University Press, 2005), p. 162.

4 Gottfried Wilhelm Leibniz, *Discourse on Metaphysics and Other Writings* (Peter Lopston ed.) (Buffalo, NY: Broadview Press, 2012), §14.

education and Wilhelm's role among the actors respond to the double manifestation according to which bourgeois had to both play a role in and watch themselves at the theatre, to know and affirm themselves as a class and thus prepare the transformation of theatre into society and of all of society into a renewed set. Alarming fissures were in fact opening up in the institutions of the aristocracy and by now every crest was metamorphosing into a mask as personality appeared on stage for what it was: a fortuitous and inessential dowry, a garb, or a veil. And it betrayed in a way that was now apparent, in addition to the stigma of class differences, that occasional air from which only Kant's radical gesture could subtract it, saving it—but now to the benefit of the bourgeoisie itself—in the domain of morality, which is both universal and necessary—and coherently founding empirical character on the intelligible, independently of space or time. The step was thus accomplished, and barely four years after the publication of the second *Critique*, Solomon Maimon could write with his usual and brilliant irreverence that one day he saw the prince Radziwill up close, 'I can't say that he arrived in his highest person [in höchsteigner Person kann ich nicht sagen] for the prince's consciousness, which is where the personality resides, had been washed away by the Hungarian wine'.[5]

On Goethe's stage, a caterpillar could transform into an aristocratic butterfly just as in real life it could have taken the place of the nobleman, if only chance had willed it. Art revealed the accidental quality of life, filling both one mask and the other with life and offered someone who could only be a caricatural personality a new and propitious occasion. To grasp it, one had to cultivate it. A new pedagogy thus arose: and articulating itself around this educational function, theatre could finally transform itself, as a 'theatralische Sendung', that is as the heart of the Bildungsroman, into true existence. That is, the life of the mask broke with its isolation in space and time in a manner that could at first seem

5 Solomon Maimon, *The Autobiography of Solomon Maimon* (Yitzhak Y. Melamed and Abraham Socher eds, Paul Reitter trans.) (Princeton, NJ: Princeton University Press, 2018), p. 47.

paradoxical: plunging into the narrative flow, making itself novel-like, immersing itself in artistic fiction. And just as Wilhelm sundered his ties with the familial realm, the theatre thus slackened even its weakest links to the material world, but only so that its new actor—the bourgeois who sees himself act not from the armchair of the theatre but from his own, holding in his hand a book—could grasp the purest and freest availability of chance, and return it superficially, on the diurnal stage of history. When dramatic tone combines with narrative flow, when one does second-degree fiction, even the costumes and the poses are sacrificed to the unreality of literary characters, but these in turn dedicate themselves to a masquerade that, no longer obscuring the real, can touch and draw on it dialectically. The weakness of representation in the face of existing relations of strength, the immateriality, that is, of the garments that the bourgeois could only occasionally put on compared with the real person that the aristocrat never ceased to be, now appears as such from the perspective granted by the novel. It both makes itself available to analysis and at the same time dissimulates itself in the fragility of the fictitious construction and does not reveal itself directly to the spectator but ever to that same bourgeois (to the reader) through the character of the bourgeois Wilhelm, a mask among others that by virtue of this double coincidence descends, so to speak, from the stage and parades and acts in the theatre of the world with an autonomy and a forcefulness that are foreign to those remaining on stage, now grown old and vague. Precisely in this sense of a coincidence in vocation of the dramatic and the narrative and of a fiction that doubles and dissimulates itself intercepting the real, or better yet of a performance that coincides with its writing and is therefore much more than a performance, one can indeed say that 'Goethe reaffirms his epoch's ideal of personality, for which his own life largely served as the model'.[6] The old, tired masks had lost their former power, transmitting it to the literary character, via a dynamic announced by the figure of Wilhelm's friend and peer, a bourgeois born

6 Adorno, 'Gloss on Personality', p. 162.

for business and incapable of forming himself, precociously greying due to the historic obsolescence and inadequacy of his role: just like the disguised men on stage, he remains deprived of a real personality. Wilhelm, however, that is, he who refuses the part assigned to his class, is the true heir of the bourgeoisie in search of affirmation. Unbeknownst to him, he has miraculously managed a decisive victory in the fight in which he has been enrolled: he, the bourgeois-actor, himself in turn a character but at the same time now more than a mask, since with him mimesis becomes a type of social education. From one's home one can thus return to one's home, and just as puppets had offered the little protagonist a first domestic theatre, or an elementary education, now it is his figure that becomes animate for the reader, who to carry out his new historic mission does not need to abandon his own affairs, follow a theatre company, and show himself on stage. Thus, Wilhelm, or anyone who by reading has been educated like him, is now capable of living at ease with chance, which no longer appears as destiny: and it can, at times, be happy. The *Bildungsroman* was precisely the expression and at the same time the realization of this dialectical process in which the mask-fiction is seemingly left to decant so that a new (theatrical but no longer merely theatrical) personality can form and in forming take shape in the single reader, or in other words in a class shaped on Goethe's model of the ascending class. By now, mimeticism itself coincided with being, and its very own subject believed itself to be much more than a mask. Maintaining or dissimulating the illusion was taken care of by the internal distinction—a new caesura, coherent with the new economic-political classification—of the figure of the inept imitator, or of the one as competent as he was untimely, that is, of the *parvenu*. And this typification of the overly-rapid ascent (or, for the observers, one beyond the time limit), is by definition a caricatural (in their eyes it represents precisely an excess) and aggressive copy, and therefore especially receptive to mythologies of race, as soon as the insecure gaze of the mimetic being has to look into that of his neighbour and rival, the protagonist of this so-called assimilation, he whom the very 'persona' of the bourgeois will be able to accuse of masked duplicity and will wish to denude (that is, deprive first and foremost of property).

If the conquest of the real world thus passed through its literary transformation, with romantic occasionalism this dynamic reaches its culmination. This moment was polemically defined by Carl Schmitt, with the commitment of someone who must conceal the masquerade he is part of, when he recalled the way Goethe represented for Novalis the greatest example of the ability to connect small and insignificant facts to important events: because life is full of chance, it resolves itself in a game, and like every game it ends with surprise and deceit. Thus, the aleatory reaches its perfect availability: according to Novalis's formula, 'all the accidents of our life are materials from which we can make whatever we want', like with Bettina von Arnim and in Schmitt's words, 'every interesting encounter becomes the occasion for a novel'.[7] By now, indeed, the implications have been drawn out: if the aristocrat was (either by birth or by chance) a person, then any chance can be a character—as long as it is worthy of interest. If it is a matter of making an occasion out of chance, some chance happenings will in any case be more fortunate than others. It is precisely when everything is mere chance that antagonism and classifications reign.

Far from denying the Kantian ideal, this dominion will impose itself precisely under its aegis: with the triumph of the bourgeois class, the universal itself or the moral person will coincide with the liberal state, which ascends, according to Hermann Cohen's formula, to a 'supreme and perfect [paradigm] of ethical self-consciousness'. We thus once again reach Marx's dictum: in the regime of competition, personality is a chance and chance a personality. In other words: chance is nothing other than the State. Incidentally, it was precisely the coincidence of the casual and the real that was claimed as such in the formula from the *Science of*

7 Carl Schmitt, *Political Romanticism* (Guy Oakes trans.) (Cambridge, MA: MIT Press, 1986), p. 83.

Logic: 'The accidental is necessary, because the real is determined as possible'. And that will once again be the case in the recent perspective offered by Odo Marquard, who will go on to extract from this schema his concept of freedom: even an arbitrary accident (that which seems choosable at will) is thus an accident of destiny, because the chance of fate throws us into a system consolidated by habits and 'we—*vita brevis*—cannot substantially change them'.[8] Here, for Marquard, the 'polychromy' of the real unfurls itself or, in other words, the variegated spectre of chance resolutions: and in truth the alternative to the 'excessive power' of a single determination is not an absence (the 'zero') but an abundance of determinants, and therefore a plural causality capable of leaving space for freedom. The multiple diverse chances mutually limit each other, defining man without imprisoning him.

Explicitly inspired by Montesquieu's doctrine of the subdivision of powers, the concept of polychromy does not hide that it subscribes to the reigning doctrine of free competition and equilibrium and that precisely towards the end of the century in which the absolutely arbitrary and the fateful had bonded in the most frightful of circumstances, instituting a power of death that only left one fortuitously alive. After this historic caesura, one might observe, the romantic canon of the 'interesting' could tacitly be replaced, as indeed happens in Marquard, with the 'dominant' of destiny that regulates the chromatic variables or delimits the same concept of freedom by transforming the casual into the factual: anyone therefore had to demonstrate themselves to be so close to death as to not have the time to eliminate the last fortuity, so that the latter could determine the life of everyone. Here, where contingency becomes clearly definitive, there is truly no more need for masks, and mimesis and being coincide without any remainder: in order to affirm itself, apologetics must not conceal but rather shamelessly exhibit its own violence.

8 Odo Marquard, *Apologie des Zufälligen: Philosophische Studien* (Stuttgart: Reclam, 1996[1986]), p. 129.

Only a revolutionary theory could therefore, against any 'dominating' pretension, reaffirm pure chance where one is supposed to encounter destiny, that is, trace back to chance the very personality of chance, conceiving of a new concept of the encounter. One must therefore evoke André Breton, and Blanchot alongside him: 'The encounter with Nadja, is the encounter with encounter, a double encounter'.[9] As such, the encounter does not in fact derive from a superiority of fate that actualizes the conjunction of two series or dynamics (a brick falls and encounters a passer-by), but designates a new, paradoxical relation, because it is precisely in the point of coincidence that non-coincidence intervenes. There is indeed

> a level of reality at which the two movements [. . .] are but two trajectories that come to intersect. Now, in this schema, what falls never kills anyone because the idea of death is not involved. To put this differently, the object as such never reaches the passer-by as such, but only an arbitrary moving object; it is *elsewhere*, in *another time* that the passer-by passes and dies . . .[10]

It is therefore the disjunction of the elements and series that does not cease to affirm itself against every destiny, for in it there is 'no relation other than the intimacy of the absence of relation'.[11]

Consider, then, the extremes. In Goethe's finale, two weddings resolve the non-coincidence of the encounter (Wilhelm and Therese) with two conjoined destinies (of Lothat and Therese, of Wilhelm and Natalie). The aleatory is here traced back to that which is destined—and personality can finally be conquered, as a *parvenu* would not know how to do—in the discovery of a common past, of the family patrimony and of hereditary resemblances (the ancient treasure of paintings belonging to Wilhelm's grandfather, the portrait of the aunt belonging to Natalie,

---

9 Maurice Blanchot, *The Infinite Conversation* (Susan Hanson trans.) (Minneapolis, MN: University of Minnesota Press, 1993), p. 413.

10 Blanchot, *The Infinite Conversation*, p. 415.

11 Blanchot, *The Infinite Conversation*, p. 417.

so similar to her, whom the little Wilhelm had met); the conquest is thus obtained at the point in which property and nature, birth and possession unite historically in the 'persona', that is, 'at the price of death's penetration into the life of the two spouses'.[12] It is thus that the book ends and its teachings are fulfilled.

In Breton, the encounter affirms on the contrary the truth of the disjunction, separating chance from death, taking one away from the other. And the 'disturbing repudiation' of Nadja's disappearance in the final pages, in favour of another figure that can be loved because it remains extraneous to the enigmatic nature of chance, keeps the latter intact beyond the book, like the risk that disturbs him because it appears with the book only to disappear and reject both destiny and the book.

39. Maine de Biran's *effort* generates personality, but only on privileged occasions, in the intimate theatre of Grateloup: in Paris, every effort becomes vain and the person loses itself in a crepuscular state. Later, Tarde will go on to elevate the somnambulist to the rank of a social man and Durkheim, according to a still-coherent development precisely opposed to the latter, will specifically exclude individuation from the characteristics of personality, which instead has a supra-individual nature.[13] He will therefore go on to confirm the 'old formula *homo duplex* [. . .] by the facts', calibrating it on the opposition of personal and social states of consciousness and assuming, as is well-known, their 'internal contradiction' as a norm or characteristic of human nature.[14] The *résistance* must then be the opposite one, in everyone, from the individual to the public, while the *effort* becomes necessary to 'résister à soi même' (resist oneself) and overcome oneself in the social sphere; and, like the

---

12 Furio Jesi, *Bachofen* (Andrea Cavalletti ed.) (Turin: Bollati Boringhieri, 2005), p. 47.

13 Durkheim, *Elementary Forms of the Religious Life*, pp. 271–72n.

14 Emile Durkheim, 'The Dualism of Human Nature and its Social Conditions' in *Essays on Sociology and Philosophy* (Kurt Wolff ed.) (New York, NY: Harper & Row, 1964), p. 328.

former, the latter will also be unceasing and destined to grow, along with the weight or action of collective being, that is, with the task that it imposes on our being 'complete'. In the late dominion of the bourgeoisie, the formation of the subject is therefore not entrusted to a stage-play or to the idleness of reading, but demands sacrifices; if man is always the same, double as before, the *caractère douloureux* of dualism shows itself now to be a 'fact': the Parisian somnambulist must suffer in order to become a person.

For his part, to conceive of the end of every effort, Bergson had to remain faithful to the principle of antagonism, translating causality into duty and chosen action: in the course of our existence—he wrote, with words similar to those of James or Pierre Janet—numerous possible personalities present themselves, which amongst themselves are 'competing rivals' and between which 'our life must choose'. Now, this very same 'choice' requires a great deal of effort, a difficult commitment that only ends with the *détente* of the dying, when chance-turned-person or rather the unity of life flows and unfolds like a panorama. Therefore, the 'moi vivant' (living I), the 'moi fondamental' (fundamental I) (and, by contrast, the suggested *moi*, the 'parasite'), the 'personnalité entière' (while personality) are terms that are coherent with the melodic duration of the past but also with the insuperable haphazardness of the end.

Such is the limit within which Bergsonism seems to be inscribed, despite its profoundly Leibnizian inspiration. One might think in this sense of the *Évolution créatrice*, of the impassioned praise of philosophy which, in attempting to reabsorb intelligence into intuition gives us the strength to truly act and live, revealing to us the intimate solidarity of the entire universe, the union of beings and their overwhelming impetus, capable of overcoming thousands and thousands of obstacles 'and perhaps even death'. The adverb describes an insuperable doubt: here, where chance erupts into the domain of finalism and the recovered melody prevails over the pre-established one, where Leibniz's force is attracted to the dominating star of consciousness and in fact 'ce flot qui monte est conscience' (this mounting swell is consciousness) (according to the

Évolution créatrice), here only the 'perhaps' reigns. Wherever the problem of personality has replaced theodicy, wherever the unity of the individual has replaced the unicity, the universality and the necessity of the supreme being, the creator of the real and the possible, beatitude becomes veiled behind uncertainty, and both hope and a certain reserve make an appearance. Indeed, the 'perhaps' corresponds to philosophy's task and weighs on this new supra-individual and unitary *effort* just as immortality can only ever be an immortality *en masse*, which demands the end of the single individual. Here, where a personality must assert itself over others, the spirit overcomes matter; where consciousness—which 'n'est pas lié [. . .] au sort de la matière cérébrale' (is not tied to the fate of cerebral matter)—is freedom itself, death does not impede but aids 'le plus grand progrès de la vie en général' (the greatest progress of life in general).[15] Thus, universal solidarity is internally animated by antagonism, by the affirmation of the present on virtual personalities and, by ending, organic life separates this world of facts from that of the *peut-être*. This domain of the hypothesis is essentially unlimited, however, or in turn hypothetical, for in it every difference between the virtual and the real disappears. Precisely the 'perhaps' is always double or self-referential, and the defeat of chance will, in turn, be an accident.

40. The death of the single individual is absorbed into the continuity of becoming, that is, into the mass that is in a constant process of formation, in which every antinomy must be resolved. This matter, however, becomes the object of Bachelard's concise criticism: for Bergson, there can be no exchanges or true fluctuations between intimate and external consciousness, only alternatives: I act and I think, I am a thing or a philosopher; and it is precisely by virtue of this contradiction that I am continuous. The general theory of *élan vital* therefore contains a doctrine of compensations which supports it, justifying the most infelicitous of initiatives, whether they be individual or especially of the entire species.

15 Bergson, *Creative Evolution*, p. 270.

And beyond the existence of the single individual, a temporal ontology unfurls itself, coherently, for which the 'duration that is full and deep, continuous and rich serves as the spirit's substance'.[16] For Bachelard, to overcome this limit, to free *durée* from the viscosity of the past, to finally render it contemporary with its own fluidity, means—as we have seen—to think a 'discontinuous Bergsonism', a dialectic of instants and intervals, a philosophy not of compensations and of melodic unity, but of interruptions and rhythms, it means refuting the dominating metaphors to recognize that continuity is not an immediate datum but a problem and a product. It means breaking with the tendency towards equilibrium and with compensatory mechanisms, to conceive of defeat and peril in their absolute and unconditional truth. According to him, Bergson did indeed show that the greatest success corresponds to the highest risk, but only by therefore assigning to the latter 'an aim and a function, [. . .] a history, a development, a logic, a myriad empirical and rational guarantees that found the continuity of the most adventurous of lives'.[17] There is, however, a pure risk, without motive, before which instinct does not retain its protective vigilance; it has a different, unrecoverable impetus, a 'strange emotional game that leads us to destroy our security, our happiness and our love, nor about the sense of exaltation that draws us to danger, newness, death, and nothingness'.[18]

Bergson had recalled and renewed the doctrine of the *petites perceptions* by declaring that men who are used to a stable conception of existence are gripped by vertigo when confronted with the sight of real duration or of 'mobilité universelle' (universal mobility).[19] Bachelard renews Bergsonism, turning his gaze toward the pulsion of death, rediscovering the instant behind *durée* and in the instant an *élan mortel* whose name once again turns out to be 'vertige'.

16 Gaston Bachelard, *The Dialectic of Duration* (Mary McAllester Jones trans.) (London: Rowman and Littlefield, 2016), p. 16.

17 Bachelard, *Dialectic of Duration*, p. 19.

18 Bachelard, *Dialectic of Duration*, p. 19.

19 Bergson, 'Perception of Change', p. 261.

41. For many deranged individuals—Moreau de Tours wrote—folly is nothing but 'la continuation d'un rêve' (the continuation of a dream).[20] For Bergson, dreams and folly are disturbances of attention to life, turmoils that affect the 'pointe' that all of our intellectual existence rests on or, in other words, the 'sensory-motor function with which it inserts itself into present reality'. To once again quote the words from *Matière et mémoire*, 'this disturbance is enough to produce a sort of psychic vertigo, and to make memory and attention lose touch with reality'. In a particularly subtle way, operating a sort of transcendence by excess, tying it to the Bergsonian adjective par excellence ('vital'), Eugène Minkowski would go on to give the expression 'contact' a renewed splendour in the history of psychopathology. ('The notion of a vital contact with reality, where the stress is to be placed on the word 'vital', has nothing to do with physiology'.[21] For his part, Bergson refers back to Moreau and cites the lectures of his student, Ball, that were based on clinical experience and on the testimonials of patients: the first manifestation of the illness, as one learns there, is often 'a sense of strangeness, or, as they say, of "unreality", as if the things they perceived had for them lost solidity and relief'.[22] On the same page of *Matière et mémoire*, one finds on the other hand a distinction that is fundamental to the economy of Bergsonism: the personality split is not a form of alienation, it is not a rupture of equilibrium or a loss of that which Ball too called the 'sentiment de la réalité' and it does not correspond to an alteration of sensory-motor functions but rather to a lessening, a weakening of the senses due to which memories lose their intimate cohesion without losing touch with the real, while memory as a unitary complex splits. Taine's conception of different personalities as groupings of ideas still appears relatively close here, in some respects. And what will surely be related to this reading is the revolutionary interpretation of Félida X's case some 20 years later, according to which the young woman's access to the existence

20 Moreau de Tours, 'De l'identité de l'état de rêve et de la folie': 373.

21 Eugène Minkowski, *La schizophrénie: Psychopathologie des schizoïdes et des schizophrènes* (Sven Follin pref.) (Paris: Payot, 1997[1927]), p. 178.

22 Bergson, *Matter and Memory*, p. 174.

that Azam considered 'secondary' depended on the exhaustion of attention to life and corresponded in reality to a pause from excessive efforts, to a period of both fatigue and recovery. The 1916 affirmation according to which 'the divided personality has essentially always been one', sounds as definitive as it is coherent with the formulation of *Matière et mémoire*. It is on the basis of the first 'doctrine of compensations' with which he builds the continuity of *durée* that Bergson can in fact re-found the person (as unitary, even if apparently divided and never multiple) in the unitary dynamic of the *élan vital*. And he can do so precisely by isolating (*pace* Pierre Janet, who had made them 'si curieusement rapprochées' [so curiously close]) the split of subjectivity from folly and vertigo. For this, he refers back to Ball's book and specifically to the pages dedicated to a grave case of *folie du doute*.

42. The victim of this singular illness is a young banker, dedicated to his work and his family, a man 'fort intelligent' though not particularly cultured. 'He has never read Descartes, or other philosophers and touches on the greatest of problems involuntarily, he does metaphysics without realizing it'. Indeed, he 'seems pursued by Cartesian doubt': he has fallen prey to a sort of universal automatic scepticism and doubts of every fact, every thing and even his very own being, without reaching the intuition of God's existence or of his own or any formal conviction to abide by.

Everything had begun on a tranquil morning in June of 1874, when the employee was as usual in his office and, all of a sudden, 'sans aucune douleur ni étourdissement' (without any pain or dizziness), the objects around him lost their familiar aspect: work instruments and equipment thus maintained their form and colour but seemed strange or even ridiculous to him, curiously deprived of relief or, as Ball glosses, of reality. The crisis, nevertheless, did not last long, and the same protagonist was able to explain it to himself by attributing it to a physiological cause. Several years later, however, in December of 1880, the illness would manifest itself again in an equally unforeseeable way and in the decidedly more acute form of depersonalization: 'I felt myself diminish, disappear.

All that was left of me was an empty body. Since then my personality has *completely* disappeared, and despite all of my attempts, I can no longer recapture this "I myself" in flight'. The sensation of estrangement is now irremissible: what is happening, the young man now asks himself. Are the things that surround me real? And who am I? Why specifically to me? 'Je existe' (I exist) is the answer, 'but beyond real life and despite myself'.

Ball does not distinguish between alienation and split personality: in fact, the formula of the *folie du doute* harkens back to the distance that now manifests itself between existence and reality and that separates (as in the case of R. L., described by Dufay) the *je* from the *moi* ('Je existe [. . .] malgré moi' [I exist . . . despite myself]). Consciousness and action appear divided and correspond to two different centres: all while finding himself in this atrocious state, the poor employee continues to behave as before and without knowing why. Something, a singular impulse that does not seem to originate from his own body, pushes him to go on, mechanically, unconsciously. Thus, he consistently fulfils his obligations, without any mistakes and yet nevertheless, although he does nothing but repeat 'I am at work, I am doing this and that', he is incapable of realizing that it is real. Recalling at least Paul Janet's observation, one might note that in R. L.'s case, too, the formula 'je existe' continues to express a feeling of pure existence. But that would equate to an overly literal understanding, as the immediate and sincere expression of that which is existentially primal, and at the same time too far from the letter, separating it unduly from the 'malgré moi'. The two affirmations are, however, indistinguishable, and the phrase 'je existe malgré moi' cannot but be pronounced in a single breath: it does not testify to a battle that has been won, but to an 'état atroce' (atrocious state), of doubt that affects the very existential primacy and that, to be exact, cannot be assigned to the pole of the *je* or to that of the *moi*. In this singular alienated idealism, there is no fundamental identity capable of resisting but merely an undefined multiplication of doubts, a *je* ever-doubled by its *moi* and projected by the *moi* and a *moi* that is in turn a spectre of the *je*:

'It seems I can sum up my situation thus: my personality has entirely disappeared; it is as if I had disappeared two years ago and the thing that exists now had nothing in common with the old "I myself"'. This surpassingly distressing condition, which can be compared to the first attacks suffered by the young Félida X (during which the most familiar of objects and faces appeared foreign and strange) is both one of depersonalization and of the subject's scission. 'It seems to me that I am dead,' explains Ball's patient, and 'yet nothing has caused my death'. That which ruptures the unity of the person is in fact a demise coherent with corporeal life, a life that now escapes, becomes automatic (or comic, as Bergson might say), foreign like that of a *moi* that cannot say 'je'. Such is the folly of doubt, the outcome of an unconscious and exasperated Cartesianism; an intolerable outcome, certainly, but also a coherent one, and a demonstration that a truly radical scepticism has overcome subjectivity, suspending every faith in its unitary appearance.

Bergson, on the other hand, argues for the continuity of the person: like Paul Janet, and like Egger, albeit in a different way. When he examines Félida's case and inverts the poles of the normal and the abnormal, he calls the second state the first and vice versa and contradicts Azam, of course, but he focuses like him on personalities A and B, ignoring the condition of intolerable unfamiliarity that precedes it. And it is precisely when he refers back to Ball that he marks his distance from him, opportunely separating folly (or 'vertige psychique' [psychic vertigo]) from the scission or multiplication of personalities, isolating the latter from depersonalization. The personality that is 'always one' does not disappear: it can reach the culmination of concentration in life and in free action by looking out towards the future, or else re-descend 'in the direction of space'—when we let ourselves go and 'instead of acting, dream', 'the self is scattered [notre moi s'éparpille]' and the past 'is broken up into a thousand recollections made external to one another'[23]—to unite in an indivisible movement before the gaze of the dying.

23 Bergson, *Creative Evolution*, p. 201.

Ball's patient, who has already disappeared before dying, will not enjoy the privilege of this panoramic vision, however. And for him no *effort* will be comparable to the extent of this loss. Having survived himself, dead and not dead, he is condemned to cohabit with a foreign himself.

43. If the *folie du doute* is, like every madness, a continuation of dreaming, only a dream seems capable of dissolving the radical doubt, overcoming every unfamiliarity. The case is a most singular one and one of the most deserving of attention: cited by Ribot in *Les maladies de la personnalité*,[24] it is taken from Daniel Hack Tuke's *Illustrations of the Influence of the Mind on the Body in Health and Disease* (1872 and 1878), translated by Victor Parant as *Le corps et l'esprit* (1886) and widely read in the circles of the *Revue philosophique* and by French psychiatry at the time. The protagonist is a doctor, who is also an alpinist. This one, however, did not miraculously save himself from a fall after having seen his entire life flash before his eyes. No, he safely reached the summit and after the enormous effort was able to enjoy a deep and well-deserved sleep. While sleeping, however, he dreamt he was falling. And in his dream, he fell, died, only to then begin, in all tranquillity, a scrupulous autopsy of his own dead body. No panoramic vision for him, therefore, or any spectacle of pure duration; and no survival of one's mortal remains for the spirit: tired of dying, exhausted in every one of its fibres, the sleeping body doubles itself in a living one, in an *alter* that is wakeful and more united than ever with the spirit. Thus, sleep ('la mort ne saurait être qu'un sommeil' [death cannot be anything other than sleep]) is dreamt, and double in dreams, and the bond of this singular *doublement* resists the decomposition of the organism.

The words used by Stefan Zweig to describe the Baron von R., who lives separately from his old I despite 'living in the lodgings of the "I" from back then and writing while seated at his desk with his pen and

24 Théodule Ribot, *Les maladies de la personnalité* (Paris: Alcan, 1883), p. 133n.

with his own hand', would certainly be fitting for Ball's doubtful employee, but they cannot be applied to Tuke's doctor, who represents instead the opposite and corresponding polarity, the case of a different revelatory dream, that arrives at the height of fatigue to illuminate active and quotidian existence. What is at stake is this: the normal life attentive to and united with the body, which requires not just rest (like Bergson's Félida) but through the dream ties its restoring sleep to the death of the body. The body of the man fallen into the ravine is obviously not the body of the doctor examining it, but at the same time it was once his. In other words, death marks the scission here between the body that I am while I look at myself and the body that I look at, or, in the terms of phenomenology, between present (including oneiric) consciousness and the reflexive I, already past, or in other words between the living, *Leib*, and the *Körper* that is mine because it belongs to my world, between touching and touched. The dream is in fact a thought in action, like the diurnal one; but for this reason, it is also revelatory: it explains to us that the only lucidity that can resist against the most extreme scepticism, the only one capable of studying the body as a thing and of thereby arranging any other thing, is precisely the one that studies and manipulates, in every object, its own abandoned remains. The doctor who carries out the autopsy in his dream thus situates himself in a position that precisely mirrors Ball's 'je existe': it is truly he who works or continues his own work, and does not suffer because he has truly become double, and does not write with the same hand 'as that I from back then', nor could he, having—beyond any doubt—his own dead body between his hands. The doctor dreamt by the doctor, the subject unveiled by his own dream, is therefore nothing other than the dream that explains itself, the finally transparent actuality of the relation to the world. And every studied body becomes in that sense the dead body doubled and separated from the living body of the one studying it, and every employment, every knowable object or tool that is manipulable—or, as one says, *vorhanden*—is offered to availability itself by spectral hands.

Thus, the alpinist from the dream, who in dreaming has duplicated and annulled the dream of doubt, the alpinist deprived of vertigo and panorama, who instead has overcome vertigo and arrived at the bottom of his precipice, is now far from Egger, Bergson and Bachelard. He is nothing other than a random doctor, who falls asleep tired every evening to awaken calmly and return to his office the next day, a man tackling his job, who examines his patience with quotidian dedication, and who can do all of this because he has separated himself from a dead body that he now scrutinizes and recognizes in the bodies of others. And everyone like him lives like him and now too he is reading or writing because he is dreaming that he has separated himself from his own remains, and thus looks at and manipulates them continuously through things and in the most diurnal familiarity. The alpinist doctor is—in other words—nothing other than the *alter ego* of Ball's *Je*, he is the *moi* that does not consider itself different in the slightest from the *je* and does not sense the atrocious experience of one who lives as if he were dead, does not suffer and macerate in doubt, but lives tranquilly thanks to the fatal fall of his double. His is indeed the quotidian dream of the world, the dream of death, of possession and habit, the common dream of a waking life that presupposes vertigo and to which one only accedes, whether one knows it or not, through vertigo.

44. The force that ties life to the body, or in other words the body's resistance, can be suspended, as Biran knew, in artificial sleep. And suspending *effort*, according to Edgar Allan Poe's famous conclusion, means stopping both life and death all at once. As in *Valdemar*, the idea is to catch the body by surprise, to make it fall asleep right when it is about to die—and then to abandon it, once it is finally exhausted. It is a matter of inducing a sort of primitive coma, perhaps so that he who inhabits the body can, in that interval without time, behold it, grasping all of that which otherwise he only possesses partially, with the only gaze that is truly without effort, that is paradoxically one's own and master of itself, since it cannot belong to the body. But for such a risky paradox it

is always too late: the point of view is both mine and not mine by definition; the gaze that one wishes to separate from the body in order to grasp it is defined by the latter and its separation is therefore a false one, or a separation from a false body that is being confused with the living one.

Returning to one of the *Marginalia* in *The Facts in the Case of M. Valdemar*, Poe mocked both the credulity and the incredulity provoked by his report, incapable of resisting or surrendering to the proof of facts that, if anything, depend on it ('Ah!—*they* are proved by *the story*'). If, of course, verisimilitude does not contradict but rather nurtures and arms fiction, this also applies precisely to Valdemar's paroxysms ('such symptoms *might* have appeared . . . '). And if facts can depend on fictions it is because the latter know how to explain the former, especially the most extraordinary and marvellous amongst them. Indeed, the plausible reference (if 'the identical symptoms *have appeared*, and will be presented again and again') it has been recognized here,[25] in a phenomenon documented by Chauncy Hare Townshend in the 1844 edition of his popular *Facts in Mesmerism*. The author, who had already accompanied the first edition (1840) with a series of authenticated testimonials, now claimed to have subjected a moribund friend of his to hypnotic treatment and to have thus prolonged his life by at least two months, although the therapy, because of certain accidental impediments, had only been started when the illness (an epidural abscess) had greatly worsened. Townshend's words ('Unfortunately [. . .] Mesmerism was not resorted to till late in the progress of the disease') are thus echoed by the famous words said by Valdemar to the hypnotizing doctor: 'I fear you have deferred it too long'. The correspondence is indeed plausible, and revealing, because it shows that the two delays have entirely different causes and natures: if the reason for one is in fact contingent, inessential and compromises a cure that, according to Townshend, would have otherwise had a favourable outcome, that of the other is by contrast necessary, essential and it does not jeopardize any therapy (Valdemar neither should nor could

25 Sidney E. Linn, 'Poe and Mesmerism', *PMLA* 62 (1947): 1093.

have been cured). If a delay owed to external causes thus compromises the outcome of Townshend's experiment, in the story recounted by Poe it is paradoxically 'late' precisely because there are no impediments, because the therapist promptly responds to the call ('You may as well come *now*') and the patient falls into a state of hypnosis at the right moment, that is, at the moment of death (' . . . do you still sleep? [. . .] Yes; still asleep—dying'). It is 'late' for Valdemar because, due to the unity of the individual and his temporal continuity, artificial sleep could truly, fully *replace* the wakeful state of the dying only if the latter were no longer such, but already dead: 'Yes;—no;—I *have been* sleeping—and now—now—*I am dead*'. The passage is famous, as is Derrida's commentary: 'The statement "I am living" is accompanied by my being-dead and the statement's possibility requires the possibility that I be dead—and the reverse [. . .] Here we understand the "I am" from the "I am dead"'.[26] From our point of view, however, an observation still seems possible: it is specifically the *homo duplex* who is a speaking corpse, *simplex in vitalitate* is both living-dead and dead-living *in humanitate*. One must not forget that Valdemar's words have a very peculiar 'sound', that—as the authentic vocal transposition of the 'données du toucher'[27]—gives the doctor the impression of a viscous and gelatinous substance. Thus, in the formula *I am dead* (where *I am* is immediately: *I am dead*), the doubleness of the subject insists on the organism itself, which in turn doubles and becomes more complicated: the living man resounds in a dead body, the dead man speaks in the living, the organic decomposes and combines with the inert element that in turn becomes living. This confusion is an exteriorization of what is internal, which now becomes apparent and involves others: the suspended intimate sense, like the *effort* in the hypnotized subject, is transposed into the doctor's

---

26 Jacques Derrida, *Voice and Phenomenon: Introduction to the Problem of the Sign in Husserl's Phenomenology* (Leonard Lawlor trans.) (Evanston, IL: Northwestern University Press, 2011), pp. 82–83.

27 Waldemar Deonna, 'Un art nouveau: Le tactilisme', *Journal de psychologie normale et pathologique* 20(1) (1923): 33.

perception, who, literally touched by that voice, hears within it the texture or resistance of fibres and flesh.

Psychologists will later go on to learn that the personality 'de conscience' can also disappear, obliterate itself, but not the one that is 'profonde et organique' (profound and organic):[28] if that which is proper to personality is, however, the body, that which still remains, which truly never manages to disappear, as Poe teaches, is a decomposing organism. The I is double because it is one, and the last sleep of consciousness remains anchored to a corpse. The force that ties life to the organism can be suspended in artificial sleep . . . and if this suspension occurs *in articulo mortis*, we will perhaps be able to discover until when we will be capable of defending property from the sorties of the last thief ('for how long a period, the encroachments of Death might be arrested by the process'). Poe's doctor thus shows, with a singular performance as a metaphysical empiricist, the truth of mesmerism: because every subject is subjected to this threat, because everyone is already old enough to die, it has always applied to the living-dead. And with the truth of hypnosis we thus also find revealed the nature of the effort that it would like to eliminate. Every force that is exerted on the resisting body, every 'immediate sense of the property of the body that is moved voluntarily' (Maine de Biran) remains in fact suspended on the death of the body and the time of *effort*, of possession or of consciousness is a prolonged instant (constitutively late) like the one that extends excessively, attaining its most acute and anguished embodiment in the pages of *Valdemar*.

When, at the end of the story, awakening is imposed by the usual mesmeric 'steps', the suspended time is reabsorbed, the normal situation restored, and the protagonist—*quia pulvis es, et in pulverem reverteris*—once again becomes himself through instantaneous decomposition. This contraction into a temporal culmination is both an exteriorization, a dispersion and an expansion into space: if, to once again use Biran's expression, the idea of the right to property was born from the immediate

28 Bernard Perez, 'Le caractère et les mouvements', *Revue Philosophique de la France et de l'Étranger* 31 (1891): 48.

sensation of the possession of the body and then extended 'to all of the external products of this activity', the gaze that the body escapes from in its own undoing is not that of the conscious subject just as it is no longer that of the dreaming I; rather, it is the gaze of another, of a doctor who, unlike his rock-climbing colleague, cannot sleep. Indeed, in the foul heap that is now before his eyes, property finally appears for what it is: the reality of many, the dream of none.

. . . A 'perhaps' weighs over survival, discontinuity (Bachelard) threatens duration. And doubt itself—that is, thought—can neither exclude nor ignore madness, but must reveal itself as radically undercut by it, and must transform itself into a 'folie du doute' (madness of doubt) because in order to endure or simply formulate oneself in an instant one must include the fatal instant. The actuality of the cogito *will certainly be lightning-quick, and in any case (since in retreating into the instant it has already given in to the enemy) not timely enough to keep death from insinuating itself in it and capturing it, and for everything to appear in a posthumous light, to a consciousness that thinsk and exists* malgré soi. *There will therefore not be any panoramic vision to enjoy and the end will not be the possibility of impossibility but the already defined dominion or the efficient norm of the possible real, that ties together and confuses therein the arbitrary and the fateful. The terror that periodically gripped Félida and the unbearable situation, the 'complete state' of Reverend Hanna now reveal their close relatedness in the words uttered by Poe's man, dead and living at the same time, a decomposing body and the consciousness of a death that has already occurred. And even if the doubt (or the Cartesian exercise) can appear false, mad, and can be suffered like a vain torment (as in the case studied by Ball) it is because the time of the* cogito, *the 'normal' time of the individual subject, is already in and of itself a time that is late,* post factum, *that in flowing dissimulates its own nature and forms our existences: in it, fear reigns and every intimidation is valid, everything can happen because it has already happened (the same need to limit retroactive violence is answered by the* Loi du 15 août 1941).

Bergson's 'peut-être' (perhaps) is inscribed on a threshold which in Minkowski's Bergsonism already becomes a caesura and a clear relation between individual life—'a life' that only death can frame and define (before death, Minkowski repeats, I see all of life, and I see the contours of a biography appear)—and 'the *life' that continues its course between 'irreparable' death and death as a vital phenomenon, between the triumphal progress of generations towards the future and the individual end, of one who dies to be such, that is, 'a being who has lived'.*[29] *The line that distinguishes existence from its negation thus repeats itself in that which isolates the singularity of* a *life from the collective unity of the living. It is in fact the same partition that doubles and explains itself: it is a peculiar distinction of death from life that by reflecting itself in that (equally characterized, historically) of the collective from the individual, immerses and bases itself in the uninterrupted event of the species. A resolution therefore had to impose itself, as a characteristic refusal of continuity, precisely in the context of Bergsonism. And Leibniz's own theory of metamorphoses—which had just been adopted and renewed—must have seemed like a veil of modesty and consolatory wisdom, draped over death and the condensation of the 'irrevocable-unrepairable'. Indeed, for Jankélévitch, death renders the totality of life irreversible: it puts an end to all becoming by breaking the metamorphic flow in which Bergson had believed (all while having to implicitly admit, though hoping and making us hope for its defeat, that death is not a pseudo-idea). And if, once again in agreement with Jankélévitch, the end of life cannot* nihiliser the fact of having lived, *the untouchable eternity of this 'having-been' (so coherent with Minkowski's 'vécu') is nothing but a gift of death itself, which cuts out 'in the infinite the biographic insularity of an existence'.* Avoir-été *therefore belongs to a life just as the living is only one who dies to be such; and if this 'quoddity' or biographic unity of the having been can be defined as an eternal instant ('fine pointe de l'instant'), it is only because death cannot annihilate that which in turn separates and produces, establishing its own domain of irrevocable appearance . . .*

---

29 Eugène Minkowski, *Lived Time* (Nancy Metzel trans.) (Evanston, IL: Northwestern University Press, 1970), pp. 131–32.

VIII

The Unforgettable

45. The experiment that tries to retain the last instant reveals the true nature of the flow of consciousness's time: indeed, there is the continuous threat, and such is the proof, or the effort, which turns every instant into a duration, and the punctual and ephemeral into a fact that is constant and, in its persistence, equal to itself. The time of consciousness is thus in arrears and continuously prolongs the past instant into the present, thus founding the unity of the subject; it is the time that continuously returns on itself (or ties itself to a non-living self), takes up or repeats itself.

We have evoked the phenomenological demand for a *cogito* without an I, a problematic and implicit demand, both indicated and betrayed by Husserl, lost in the 'essential insoluble problem'[1] of the constitution of the self, and which can be granted by the 'miracle'[2] of the *epoché* only because the latter 'must *persist*', thus doubling the continuity of the ego in a disinterested, unnatural attitude that is nevertheless fatally tied, precisely because it *maintains itself* in its isolation, to the changing but unitary series of acquisitions and sedimentations of the I. The attempt made by the young Sartre to save a pure, transparent and impersonal consciousness by isolating it from the figure of the transcendental ego finds

1 Jan Patočka, *Die Bewegung der menschlichen Existenz: Phänomenologische Schriften II* (Klaus Nellen, Jiří Němec and Ilja Srubar eds) (Stuttgart: Klett-Cotta, 1991), p. 280.

2 Jean-Paul Sartre, *The Transcendence of the Ego: A Sketch for a Phenomenological Description* (Andre Brown trans.) (London: Routledge, 2004), p. 28.

its limit here. Sartre can indeed criticize Husserl by opposing him to Husserl (deploying the *Logische Untersuchungen* and the lectures on *Zeitbewusstsein* against the *Ideen*) and refute the 'superfluous and harmful' ego while remaining faithful all the same to the fundamental idea of intentionality. The 'unifying and individualizing' I, the 'producer of interiority' then appears as a redundant (and therefore false and deceiving) projection, because consciousness itself, by virtue of its intentional structure already 'transcends itself [. . .] unifies itself in fleeing itself [. . .] perpetually refers back to itself' and 'whoever says "a consciousness" speaks of every consciousness and this singular property belongs to consciousness itself'. If this rigorously phenomenological conception can demonstrate the uselessness of the 'unifying and individualizing *I*',[3] it is because pure and impersonal consciousness already possesses the fundamental character of personality and indeed so decisively as to produce it and render it—ever *in the context of consciousness itself*—superfluous. What is therefore at stake is not a fundamental ego that persists despite the mutations of the external one but specifically, even before that, the identity of consciousness (or its permanence) to which the former harkens back. It is precisely here, in other words, where the ego becomes useless, that, along with intentionality, the old idea of the consequentiality of the *cogito* remains valid—the same one that Husserl had rethought in the innovative sense of retention, but which Brentano had already redefined in those pages of the *Psychologie von empirischen Standpunkt* (1874), considered by James to be the best ever written on the unity of consciousness: what counts is therefore the idea that in every single *cogitatio* the preceding one continues its course. To conceive of a consciousness emancipated from the ego, Sartre must base himself on the Husserlian interpretation of the *Zeitbewusstsein*, or of the unification of lived experiences that does not need a subject or an ulterior flow.

3 Sartre, *Transcendence of the Ego*, p. 3.

Now, one might observe in Deleuze's footsteps, that precisely the idea of the centred unity of the flow of consciousness fatally brings with itself the hypostasis of the I-pole. To free oneself from this continuity, one would instead have to conceive the figure of a consciousness—if one can use this term, as Walter Benjamin noted, depriving it of every subjective element—that is not retentional (and without extension), that is not constitutively in arrears (or ahead) of itself, that does not need to tie itself to itself in order to not disappear in an anonymous, unrecoverable instantaneity, that is therefore neither a *continuum* of punctual actions nor a discontinuous punctuality. Husserl himself affirms, however, that consciousness is originally and immediately self-consciousness (and therefore does not comport an infinite regression): it presides not only over the I but over retention itself and therefore does not depend on it. Perhaps it consequently remains possible to isolate a non-retentional transparency, a time, in other words, that does not refer back to any centrality or continuity. We could also define it not as the time of an impersonal consciousness (as in Sartre), but—in an ever more approximate and seemingly paradoxical manner—of a personality that cannot be referred back to a consciousness or to itself, without a remainder or in other words that is absolute.

46. 'Not all of Dr Sidis's positions convince me, but I can wholeheartedly recommend his interesting and instructive, not to mention extremely original treatise'. With these words, James concluded his introduction to the *Psychology of Suggestion* (1898), the first results of the patient experiments designed and conducted at Harvard and later in New York by the great psychiatrist who, having arrived in the United States ten years earlier, fleeing from pogroms, had been a brilliant student of his. James had remained in close contact with Sidis during the writing of this work; he had witnessed the development of his views and not all of them, it is true, had convinced him. The theoretical pivot of the book was indeed the concept of personality, which Sidis had rethought in an innovative manner, through a rigorous critique of James's own conception.

'It is clear already that the margins and outskirts of what we take to be our personality extend into unknown regions,'[4] James had written in 1895, regarding cases of doubling, indicating the exploration of these areas as the most urgent task for psycho-pathological research. Already in the well-known chapter on the 'stream of consciousness' in *Principles of Psychology* (1890), he had recognized in the concatenation of thoughts the central nucleus of personality, which possesses all of its characteristics: every *cogitatio* therefore tends towards the personal form, attaining it or remaining in the sphere of subconscious thoughts—evident in a state of suggestion or hysteria—which do not communicate with the normal self but can instead form secondary units or personalities.

For his part, in Chapter XIX of the *Psychology of Suggestion*, titled precisely 'The Problem of Personality', Sidis asks himself whether the subconscious that suggestive treatment uncovers beneath 'upper consciousness' is or is not a personality. In order to give an answer, he observes, one must first ask the preliminary question: 'What is personality?' Ignoring the metaphysical theories of the soul or the transcendental I, he naturally turns to the 'great revolution toward empiricism' that had untied the person from the role of substantial principle to see it as a directly verifiable phenomenon: he thus cursorily analyses James Mill's associationist theory and, underscoring that the tying together of senses in a single series still remains unexplained there, he takes up and appropriates a critical observation made by James to then contest the latter's very conception of personal identity, based on the stream of consciousness or on 'wave theory'. James, Sidis observes, rightly opens up a breach in the construction of associationists and yet nevertheless, even postulating that every single moment of consciousness contains the synthesis of all others, he continues to conceive of personality as a series and as a function of memory. Every thought can thus contain within it the preceding ones, but the present moment of consciousness remains, as James

4 William James, 'Person and Personality: From Johnson's *Universal Cyclopaedia*' in *Essays in Psychology* (Cambridge, MA: Harvard University Press, 1983[1895]), p. 321.

writes in the *Principles*, harkening back to Richard Hodgson, 'the darkest in the whole series', that is—Sidis once again comments—obscure to itself and it can only be know 'when dead, when it has become a content of a succeeding wave of consciousness'.[5]

Personality is not, however, a *continuum* of conscious moments, it is not their unity or synthesis in a temporary thought but rather, essentially, self-consciousness, and even if one posits a continuity or series, for Sidis 'the present moment of self-consciousness' is 'certainly the brightest of all'. This perfect overturning of James's formula implies a radical consequence: 'We can conceive of an eternal moment of self-consciousness with no preceding moment to synthesize and, indubitably, such a moment of self-consciousness is in itself a personality'. This will be a consciousness devoid of memory or identity ('because they are superfluous, since there is no preceding series to synthetize'), certainly, and yet nevertheless, or rather for that very reason, it will have the purest personal form. It is precisely the single flash of consciousness, 'not owned' by the next moment, that is thus 'the perfect person'.

Against Sartre's strategy, which rejects the I and the person to affirm a consciousness that nevertheless retains the character of unitary continuity, it thus seems possible to isolate—at least as the final, 'purely hypothetical' stage of a series that is in turn 'hypothetical', which from the 'desultory consciousness' of invertebrates goes via the 'recognitive consciousness' of superior animals all the way to the 'disconnected' or 'synthetic' consciousness of man—a conscious figure that is absolutely unrelated, which can in other words be rigorously called a 'person' without having an identity or biographical story associated with it. In other words, conceiving of the mask or the person in its purity means untying it from any relation to the continuity (empirical or transcendental) of its bearer, that is, from any relation of possession: the mask is not an

5 Boris Sidis, *The Psychology of Suggestion: A Research into the Subconscious Nature of Man and Society* (William James intro.) (New York: D. Appleton and Company, 1903), p. 192.

artificial or false identity, made to conceal one's character or personality—the blush on one's face, as Descartes said—but coincides with the simple, instantaneous presence of the latter, finally untied from the unitary synthesis of past moments. Now, that which normally ties this 'more luminous' moment to the series of other, non-present, dead ones, thus making it paradoxically 'the most obscure' one of all, is called—in James's terms—habit. 'Enormous fly-wheel of society, its most precious conservative agent' (James), in the Jamesian schema it not only remains far from anonymous automatism and directly or positive connected to personality, but at the same time it ensures the true continuity of consciousness: it ties its every moment to others, keeping them in a single 'chain' even when attention disappears (and which would immediately be reactivated if habit were erroneously contradicted). If once again in the famous pages of *Principles of Psychology*, James therefore defines *habitus* as an overcoming of resistances made possible by our organism's plasticity or capacity for adaptation (or the apparatus of reception and transmission of stimuli), the theory of states of consciousness is thus reduced to the continuity of an education, which makes the nervous system into our ally rather than our enemy: cultivating habit means handing over to the 'effortless custody of automatism' the majority of our activities so that our mental powers, freed of this weight, can freely and fully develop. But precisely this absence of effort, this disattention or rather this passive, involuntary, unreflected attention requires daily care, a particular asceticism, informed by a series of norms, the last of which says: keep the faculty of making an effort alive in yourself. Attention and effort are synonyms, but the habit that placates effort is a modality of attention. While a logical circle encloses and protects the *continuum* of phases of consciousness, personal identity—conceived in terms of flow, of series, of memories of states—can empirically be conserved through constant exercise and thus associated, once again on this plane, with the dynamic of effort and resistance.

In Sidis, however, everything changes, and the definition of self-consciousness as pure personality (the sixth and last stage of his hypothetical classification) presents a significant connection to the 'desultory self-consciousness' (the fourth stage), devoid of synthesis, describable as a series of discontinuous, unstable personalities, which like strange 'bubbles' float up to the surface from the depths of the unconscious and dissolve without leaving a trace. Made up of a multitude of moments, this type of self-consciousness does not preserve, however, any memory of the sequence itself nor can it therefore adhere to a personal identity. The lack of memory and the absence of identity are thus common characteristics of the 'perfect person' stage and at the same time basic deficiencies, if (negatively) associated with the series. The latter can be appreciated if its every moment is synthetically included in the following one, as habitually occurs in human mental activity (the fifth level, peculiar to James, of synthetic self-consciousness), or it can exist while remaining unknown, as happens with multiple or disparate personalities. In the pure form of personality, on the other hand, 'there is no series; it is but one moment'. This is a stage (as logic would demand, a 'purely hypothetical' one) devoid of identity and memory, which have neither multiplied nor split, which have not been confused or lost but which have simply become superfluous, along with continuity or with the series itself.

The perfect person, Sidis's pure personality, does not therefore have the characteristics of the synthetic one, but maintains those of the disjointed personality, transforming and overturning them *in bono*, freeing them in other words from the principle of the mnemic *continuum*: one may therefore also define it as a 'desultory self-consciousness' finally liberated from the succession of appropriations or the 'chain' that human consciousness habitually synthesizes and constructs on the foundations of identity. Developing Sidis's idea, it seems licit to imagine, in other words, that the sixth stage is nothing other than the fourth in the absence of habitual synthesis, that is to say, that the fourth appears 'disjoined' only in the presence of synthetic activity and that the latter is therefore tied to the very same disintegration of the unconscious into a series of inconsequential personalities. In any case, the theoretical shift from the fourth to the sixth state does not imply a transition into the (synthetic) fifth but rather, so to speak, an essential jump that avoids it. How is one to understand this non-passage? If for James the concatenation of thought is the nucleus of consciousness and of personality, if every thought therefore tends, in synthesis, towards the form of personal identity and unlinked thoughts remain in the unconscious as mere secondary units, it is—once again—only beyond the principle of concatenation that the 'disjointed personality' itself can shine through in the pure form of consciousness, that is, as a perfect person. And considering the role that James attributes to habit and to education as well as to their link with synthetic consciousness or personality, we could respond that the transformation of the 'desultory' condition into the perfect one demands the cancellation not only of the synthesis but of the series itself or of habitual mental activity for the sake of a counter-education or of an entirely new education.

47. In 1911, Sidis entrusts to the pamphlet *Philistine and Genius*—inspired by the experience of his son, the famous *enfant prodige* William James Sidis—his irrevocable indictment of the school system, a model of evaluation and instruction 'which Professor James, in a private conversation with me, has aptly defined as "idiotic"'.[6] Sidis observes that schooling cultivates *routine*, rewards mediocrity, stupidity and subordination, producing inveterate philistines, men ready to immolate themselves on the field of battle, and it can therefore essentially tolerate anything with the exception of genius, which must necessarily be considered abnormal. The reference to the tribulations of the prodigiously intelligent Billy is entirely transparent:

6 Boris Sidis, *Philistine and Genius*, 2nd EDN (Boston: Richard G. Badger, 1917), p. 48.

> A principal of a high school in one of the prominent New England towns dismisses a highly talented pupil because, to quote verbatim from the original school document, 'He is not amenable to the discipline of the school, as his school life has been too short to establish him in the habit of obedience.' 'His intellect,' the principal's official letter goes on to say, 'represents a marvel to us, but we do not feel, and in this I think I speak for all, that he is in the right place.' [. . .] A superintendent of schools in lecturing before an audience of 'subordinate teachers' told them emphatically that *there was no place for genius in our schools.*[7]

Sidis follows and radicalizes James's concepts. He bases himself on the latter's idea of plasticity, but only in order to untie it from the connection with habit, which tends on the contrary to harden. One could say instead that as soon as a habit manifests itself, a plasticity is lost to *routine*. A child, on the other hand, is the most plastic and least habitual subject there is. And no child is abnormal, because there is genius in every child: 'Plasticity of mind,' Sidis writes in the appendix to the second edition of the book, 'is characteristic of genius. Plasticity of mind and body is pre-eminently characteristic of the child.'[8] School education, which begins very late in a child's life, must therefore be replaced by a precocious, pre-scholastic education, capable of nurturing the plasticity of the child's dispositions before these are formed and habits take root. Now, *Philistine and Genius* is an educational pamphlet, written for parents and whose theoretical tone we have just hinted at. But the direction is clear and precise. Sidis refers back to the results of his own research and evokes psychopathological science, which established a principle of the greatest importance not only in clinical therapy but also in the field of education proper: 'it is the principle of stored up, dormant, reserve-energy,—the principle of potential, subconscious, reserve energy.'[9] Usually

7 Sidis, *Philistine and Genius*, pp. 46–47.

8 Sidis, *Philistine and Genius*, p. 118.

blocked, these latent forces can freely emerge if a loosening of inhibitions occurs in the patient by means of a specific educational technique. One might recall the case of Reverend Hanna, his amnesia, his entrance into an infantile condition, that of a child gifted with a brilliant quickness of learning, and therefore the appearance of the 'primary state', of the educated adult personality, isolated from and in conflict with the other. The method by which Sidis succeeds in making the first personality emerge and thus in patiently reintegrating and combining the two is based not on hypnosis (which would have been impossible, in the case of the immune Hanna), but on a semi-conscious or "hypnoidal" condition, that is, the state of extreme relaxedness that precedes sleep or awakening but can nevertheless be induced, a state during which 'bits, mere fragments of the past experiences' appear, ready (exactly like bubbles that make contact with air) to disappear from consciousness right after their appearance. In this crepuscular state 'the subconscious primary personality must be stimulated, brought to the surface as often as possible and finally the two personalities must be merged into one'.[10] The fragment by fragment reconstruction of the entire personality therefore corresponds to the cure of the sick adult and, at the same time, to the education of the brilliant child.

Philosophy of personality, clinical practice and theory, as well as pedagogical practice reveal themselves to be rigorously intertwined. And Sarah Mandelbaum Sidis entrusted to her memoirs a didactic illustration of the binding connection between educational learning and the relaxation produced by the condition of hypnosis:

> Boris was the first to treat patients by inducing this state. But mothers who have talked and read little stories to their children to make them fall asleep, their minds full of wonder and happiness, have known it for generations. It is what I too tried to do with Billy during the first years, all while understanding how

9 Sidis, *Philistine and Genius*, p. 56.

10 Sidis and Goodheart, *Multiple Personality*, p. 160.

> important it was to avoid banal stories that were full of commonplaces or unpleasantnesses. Finding the tales of the Grimm Brothers sombre and those of Hans Christian Andersen sad and melancholy, I turned to Greek myths, which became Billy's first night-time stories' (Mandelbaum Sidis).

If in the course of psychiatric therapy the unconscious personality emerges, approaches the surface, and can be controlled and guided, if the educational exercise can meld the two rival Hannas into a single person, it is because the secondary infantile consciousness is not hardened in infantile attitudes or poses but remains extremely plastic and disposed to welcome or develop the fragmentary, still potential moments of personality. The child must therefore be educated so that those things which remain hidden and inhibited within him can reveal and free themselves. True pedagogy is thus nothing other than relaxation and disinhibition or the destruction of habits. It is a precocious, pre-scholastic education that rejects the banal and the repetitive as being repugnant and sad, that does not cultivate habit or induce automatism, that does not render effort ordinary but, replacing the latter (that is, the principle of action) or resistance with "plasticity", breaks the series, opening it up to the unforeseeable. Now, how is this plasticity freed and maintained? The method is destructive. The power of breaking up habits—as one reads in *Philistine and Genius*—is the essential factor of a good education, the key capable of freeing the reserves of otherwise inaccessible self-conscious energy: 'The cultivation of the power of habit-disintegration is what constitutes the proper education of man's genius'.[11]

The continuity of the personal ego is produced and maintained by a circularity of attention and habit. This circle is the fly-wheel of the social apparatus. Relaxation dissolves instead the infinite elasticity of the mind, liberates intellectual potentialities from regulated concatenations and can therefore elude, or to use the exact words, 'may transcend the synthetic personality', and thus the very same normal/abnormal partition,

11 Sidis, *Philistine and Genius*, p. 60.

immediately transforming the disjointed and fragmentary moment of consciousness into the moment of the genius or the perfect person, which is that of a pure, irresistible, and unrelated self-consciousness, capable of not habituating itself to anything because it does not have to make an effort for anything.

In that precise moment, the difference between the unconscious and consciousness disappears, and one can affirm, as William James Sidis himself demonstrated in an article from 1914, 'Unconscious Intelligence', that there is a properly unconscious intelligence, or rather that the latter does not differ from consciousness. Consciousness (or rather, in Boris's terms, self-consciousness, a pure personality without identity or memory) is alive in me even when I do not recognize it, and even *unconscious processes are conscious*. If during a walk—to cite the direct experiences of the then 16-year-old author—the *Aeneid* comes to my mind and I think of 'alma Venus', focusing on the first words, and therefore asking myself the reason for this unexpected thought, I discover not far away a building called 'The Alma', or if I pass through a square with the shop window of a bookstore in the distance and later in dreaming I see a book with indistinguishable letters on the cover, or if I continue to repeat two stanzas of verse that nobody but my unconscious could have composed, it means that an unconscious intelligence possesses the faculties of memory and reasoning or, in other words, that nothing distinguishes it from consciousness. William James Sidis affirms that 'the existence of a consciousness is not disproved by the lack of direct evidence,' and continues with a reference to intersubjectivity and an analogy that seems almost Husserlian in tone:

> I have no direct evidence of the consciousness of the persons with whom I speak: but yet they act precisely as if they were conscious, and I am thus led to infer that they are so. Similarly, if I see actions in my own body which I myself have nothing to do with (at least apparently), but which are precisely those kinds of actions that are produced by consciousness, I must infer that

> there is one more consciousness existent in me [. . .] to deny consciousness where there is no direct evidence is to construct a sort of solipsism.[12]

Thoughts and involuntary, automatic actions accomplished in a somnambular state are thus conscious; the genius lives in a hypnoidal state, and the moment that precedes or follows sleep extends for him to the entire state of wakefulness and merges with oneiric activity: the *homo duplex* is no longer divided *in humanitate* between the states of wakefulness and sleep, activity and passivity, between the personal and the impersonal, Grateloup and Parisian somnambulism. And if we can conceive of a unity of the human beyond any effort, then corporeal life and simplicity *in vitalitate* must also be rethought. If wherever the principle of *effort* (and therefore of the will) reigns, relaxation can seem like the product of habit or automatism, one must instead recognize in it a property of consciousness, to think a complete consciousness or a perfect personality, without memory or identity. The model is thus once again infantile genius: when we look at children playing, Boris Sidis observes, we primarily note that they lack any consciousness of effort, which would only appear through an inveterate mistake of ours ('Even if there is any effort present it is only for the observer: the child that carries out the game has no consciousness of effort')[13]. Indeed, the effort stretches out the instant of consciousness into a persistent continuity, which will in turn impose new labours: a continuous *dressage*, directed at producing the socially normal individual by connecting every time the flywheel of habit to the mechanism that captures and disjoins genius from man. But a counter-exercise remains possible: the very unconsciousness of the effort becomes consciousness, in which everything is brilliantly transformed into play. Only play, in fact, destroys *routine*.

---

12 William Hames Sidis, 'Unconscious Intelligence' in Boris Sidis, *Symptomatology, Psychognosis, and Diagnosis of Psychopathic Diseases* (Boston: Richard G. Badger, 1914), pp. 436–37.

13 Boris Sidis, *The Psychology of Laughter* (New York: D. Appleton and Company, 1913), p. 11.

48. The instantaneous position of the ego as a thinking being distinguishes it from the extension of matter and precisely this radical separation of the body from the soul implies in Descartes that their union can only be attributed to a divine will and at the same time that the psychology of man, as it results from this union, is not purely spiritual but is 'corrompue par le corps' (corrupted by the body).

With the 'original Cartesian foundation of the entire epoch of modern philosophy' (Husserl) what therefore imposed itself was the necessity to isolate from psychology a purely spiritual speculative life, one that was in turn emancipated from the animal, physical and biological body. The phenomenological principle of the pure 'I' comes to life in this scenario, much like the conceptual line drawn through the Husserlian distinction of the *Leib* from the *Körper* by Merleau-Ponty's *chair*. We are dealing with a series of figures that are still coherent with that moment of inaugural valorization (of the spirit) that defines man as a thinking being, distinguishing him from the animal-machine. Since then, the first separation (of the *res cogitans*) has had to be extended every time to the second one (of the human from the animal) while the latter insisted on the former, assigning ahead of time to the *cogito* the role of the master dealing with a biological life that in serving him separates itself from him and therefore dictates its own conditions. In the meantime, the purity of thought acquired an ethical aspect, which simultaneously distinguished it from the obscurity of the passions but also betrayed the (negative, tacit or paradoxical) relation that every morality has with the animal economy.

The formula *homo simplex in vitalitate et duplex in humanitate* presents and sums up precisely the two co-essential phases of the division of substances and of the devaluation of simple life; it expresses the hierarchy, the dominion and at the same time the unity of the dominator and the dominated. And in the meantime the Cartesian function become explicit: the position of the thinking substance is distinguished from the body and at the same time, for this very reason, it refers and ties itself to the body, it is *simplex* when it is *duplex*. An individual egoity, which finds itself assigned an organism that dies and that in separating itself thus from others will always remain *a* body, thereby polarizes itself: individuality implies a duplicity that is in turn doubled by the biological simplicity from which it separates itself. Now, if the simple life separated from conscious humanity is also shared by the latter, nothing guarantees that consciousness will situate itself on one side or the other of this divide. Hence, in naked existence it can appear drowsy or it can suddenly awaken. Such is the case of somnambulism: when its corporeal double falls asleep, consciousness can awaken in simple life without consciousness. Its ambivalence thus requires a new magic that is capable of controlling it, which, in the full dominion of energy theories, takes the name of animal magnetism, of mesmerism. But—as the contemporaries of Maine de Biran, Charles de Villers, Joseph Philippe François Deleuze or the Marquis of Puységur well knew—it manifests itself and draws its strength from the very same 'force de la volonté' (strength of the will) that opposes it, acting therefore on the body to hold back and govern consciousness. The real issue at stake, which is entirely political, was immediately obvious, and the magic itself had to in turn be controlled, reduced to the laws of science, or rather replaced by science: modern psychiatry was born out of the end of mesmerism, and the theory of double personalities was born out somnambulism. A new discipline decreed that the normal individual is one who has *a* life producing this unity from multiplication, and in the meantime the 'fonction biographique' (biographical function), which was originally applied to gods and heroes, was not merely spreading among common men but—as Pierre Janet noted—became a social demand and injunction. Like the control of personality, the telling of a life is an arduous undertaking, with always butts up against the ancient objection of empiricism. On this topic, Janet cites Proust, notably the Duchess of Guermantes who appears to her admirer in three different persons, or the proliferation of internal characters to whom the narrator himself must every time announce the death of Albertine: and he admits that a gap remains unbridgeable, he recognizes 'un grand vague dans cette fonction biographique, dans cette fonction de décrire notre personnalité propre' (a great vagueness in this biographical function, in this function of describing our own personality).[14] The construction of a past that belongs to us is a labour worthy of Sisyphus, but 'society acts on us and dictates difficult tasks' and so friends will notice with disappointment that we forget important happenings, while 'the police demands an ever-more-detailed *curriculum vitae*; this is imposed upon us, and so we make an effort that can be made easier by our literary education'.

The formational novel (its writing) and the formation (in reading) of bourgeois personality are thus connected with the history of the police as an institution and a lengthy, tiresome exercise selects the 'normal' individual, that is to say one capable of drawing up correctly and accurately his own biography every time (Janet), forming new guardians of the self, ever more naturally inclined towards self-filing. The biographic function intersects at a certain point with the Goethean function, articulating and building the personality around the great void of consciousness or the abyss of causality opened up by simple animal life. Destined for Paris, the biography can absorb—and ideally sums up—the entire work of Grateloup: indeed, it does not suffer the defeat of the diary, because it is the very power that weighed menacingly over that book that lent form to its subject. Although they cannot comprehend the entirety of life from birth to death, autobiographies, as well as the biographies of common individuals, have in fact been influenced since antiquity by the model of the first biographies of gods and heroes, who 'were born and never died, or at least they suffered a death that was merely the beginning of a new period of activity':[15] any fragmentary nature therefore remains

14 Pierre Janet, *L'évolution psychologique de la personnalité: Compte-rendu intégral des conférences d'après les notes sténographiques* (Miron Epstein ed.) (Paris: Chahine, 1929), p. 525.

15 Arnaldo Momigliano, *Lo sviluppo della biografia greca* (Turin: Einaudi, 1974), p. 14.

foreign to these writings, their form is always finite. The same disposition consequently lives on in the modern version: when the biographic function coincides with the social one, every moment appears in the light of definitive completion because my point of view as a normal subject is the same as the non-mine, supra-individual one *par excellence*, and the time of personality (heredity and concreteness of the *cogito*) always by definition remains in arrears with respect to itself, behind itself, present and dated; and the time of the 'entire life' reveals itself to be mutable but ever objective to every gaze.

49. Once again, and every time aside from Descartes, we find the spirit and the mechanism, intelligence and self-consciousness, the opaque mass of the resisting organism and, precisely, the effort at odds with one another. Of course, the Cartesian position conceived of the union or very close bond ('corpus [. . .] cui mentis sit ita conjuncta', 'corpus quod mihi *valde arcte conjunctum* est') as a being, and the distinction was not strictly reducible to a relation of property. 'Of course,' as Nancy rightly observed, 'I *am* a thinking thing, while I *have* a body. But I *am* united to this body. The closeness of the union, its tightening (*valde arcte*), its *permixtio*, means precisely that it cannot be reduced to an extrinsic relation of having.' Unless, he goes on,

> Descartes introduces here the general question of the *being of having*, of the being of property as possession, a question that remains to be extracted from a whole tradition (philosophical, political, economic) for which being as property (and also under the form of 'one's own body' or the 'body proper') is opposed to the impropriety of having.[16]

One might perhaps observe here that 'one's own body' is inseparable not only from possession but from having itself, not only from *habitus* as acquisition and dominion of consciousness but from its present constitution . . . One must return to Maine de Biran, however, to note that

16 Nancy, *Ego sum*, p. 96.

he remains faithful to Cartesianism when he takes up Boerhaave's formula and founds a philosophy of the being of property, in the name of *effort*. It is once again in this sense—and one must insist on this point—that with the notion of 'force hyperorganique' (hyper-organic force) he can confer what ends up being an ontological tone to the energetic theory of the preceding century. If the antinomic element of energy is in fact inertia, energy is still a force, and in its presentness it always encounters an opposite force, or a resistance. Now, the antinomy of what resists is not that which yields, but that which is neutral. This was already clear in the eighteenth-century conception, which was both an aesthetics and a political theory (Michel Delon) capable of conceiving of a series of pure conductors of socially prevailing forces, ordaining arts and *mores* to these as well as guiding habits. Thus, in architecture, for example, a barracks had to transmit a certain social energy, in other words, it had to possess a fitting *caractère* that would be coherent with a severe Tuscan order and which a Corinthian frieze, as refined as it is incongruous, would have contradicted, exposing the martial world to ridicule and fatally weakening the entire building, thus impeding and deviating like a resistance or a *sabot* the ordinary flow of civilization and education. Political energy, in other words, does not just spread and penetrate the social body, thereby lending it shape, but depends on and derives from its conductors, from their coherent construction—or from their neutrality: on its own, the simple absence of resistances constitutes in fact a perfect transmission or selection of the dominating power. But not only that: this political or social energy which consists in its diffusion encounters true resistance in the body and manifests itself in this encounter, that is, in the physiologies of temperament, producing individualities and modelling consciences. Indeed, it is certain that in encountering the tenaciousness of the organism (that which is not yet neutral, that which is not yet completely built), force shows and defines itself as *effort*: to return to the example of the barracks, this power simultaneously impresses and manifests itself—it is precisely a character—through its conductors, and in transmitting itself it forms the body, postures, habit and consciousness, that very same personality or martial spirit (which are later revealed in faces or handwriting precisely because these are merely imprints, traces or physical traits of the social energy—this is the *a posteriori* reason for physiognomy). If there is thus an internal *effort*, one that is autonomous and neutral with respect to the social forces that guide the Parisian somnambulism, it is only because neutrality is the force itself and interiority is merely a dissimulated exteriority. Where force encounters resistance, in other words, the individual is produced as the subject of a habituation (and the brain, as in Bergson, can appear as an 'organe de pantomime', a mediator between thought and the body): not a simply passive subject, but one endowed with will and the ability to act. It is precisely at this meeting-point, in fact, that Maine de Biran shed light on an ulterior articulation, distinguishing activity from passivity and recognizing, with the concept of *habitude active*, the will in habit itself: it is precisely with the idea of a hyper-organic force that he brilliantly defined the non-external and inapparent way in which the organism manages to intercept an energy that in the meantime transforms itself, in the 'state of force', into individual consciousness.

If the energetic theory can be welded onto the theory of consciousness in an ontology of property, it is thus in the name of corporeal resistance and of 'that which is called "force", "effort", "conatus", from which action itself must follow if nothing prevents it'.[17] With the grafting of the Leibnizian principle of force onto the figure of the *cogito*, the 'profound and paradoxical' (Wahl) Cartesian theory of the union of the soul and the body now finds a coherent solution: the spiritual is held to the organic, the punctual time of the act prolongs itself by spreading via the extension of internal space, and force becomes the *effort* or will of the individual: 'le type complet et l'abrégé' (the complete type and the synopsis) (Ravaisson) of a consciousness that by now cannot be reduced to an act of thinking. But Biran's philosophy is not a monadology . . .

---

17 Leibniz, *Theodicy*, §87.

50. Rethinking and solving this conjunction means once again turning to Leibniz. As the condensed expression of consciousness, *effort* is indeed the awakening of consciousness, and awakening means self-evidence, identification, and self-possession. The *cogito*, on the other hand, can translate into *effort* if consciousness is apperception: thus Biran's somnambular state corresponds, in Leibnizian terms, to the 'multitude des perceptions où l'esprit ne distingue rien' (multitude of perceptions in which the soul cannot make anything out), which causes vertigo and resembles death, while *compos sui* equates to the reflexive consciousness of this internal state, which 'n'est point donnée à toutes les âmes, ni toujours à la même âme' (is not given to all souls, or always given to the same one). The indubitable fact clings to the body, the being of thought becomes the being of property, force captures and produces individuality, the *je* adapts to its name, the single event or the retained instant of apperception and memory itself extend into personal biography. But we should remember Renouvier's objection: if vertigo strikes us, it is because the *effort voulu* and the *sensation musculaire* are not immediately united, as Maine de Biran might have thought, and instead there remains 'an essential element separating them: the imagination of the foreseen movement'.[18] As Renouvier explains, 'mental vertigo' is precisely this type of element, that is, the disposition to realize that which is imagined, in fact that which is most powerfully imagined, which is to say that which is most feared. Now, from our point of view, this theory reveals that the connection between force and *cogito* is possible due to the ideodynamic and magical tone of the latter: that is, the insidiousness of the *ergo* resides in the vertiginous definition not only, as Sartre has shown, of the I as the useless and degraded product of consciousness, but of consciousness that confirms itself (this is its constitutive delay) as the consciousness of an imagined ego projected by thought. It is precisely this egocentric and whirling structure—not a syllogism but a logical vertigo—that demands

---

18 Charles Renouvier, *Traité de psychologie rationnelle d'après les principes du criticisme*, VOL. 1, Essais de critique générale, VOL. 2 (Paris: Colin, 1912), p. 261.

appropriation as its Sisyphean labour and that must anchor itself in a body always already exposed to the threat and old enough to die.

There is, however, a theory of genius, or of play, that does not isolate biographical identity and overcomes the appearance of the end by returning even subconscious processes to consciousness, such as stupor and sleep, rousing reserves of energy from any 'état d'assoupissement' (state of lethargy), whether it be induced by death or some other accident.[19] For this different vision it will not be strange if those who draw on these new sources manage to dance, to ride with their closed eyes and to play cards while discussing therapies with doctors, or rather the evolution of their own somnambulism.

This theory breaks or, better yet, distorts the Leibnizian concatenation precisely at the point in which animal life, endowed with memory rises to the properly human level of personal identity and of the immortality of the soul, and attributes instead an indestructible character to memory, an immortal nature not to the soul but to life itself. It recognizes an unforgettable life without memory and a moment which is also unforgettable, which must not extend into effort and remains extraneous to the threat of death, because in its case—to use Benjamin's words—'here it is not a question of duration' and immortality 'has nothing to do with immortality in the usual sense' which believes life to be passing and instead considers immortal 'the flesh, energy, person, spirit in their various guises'.[20]

The Leibnizian terminology ('monade nue', 'bloße Monade', 'simple monade', 'simple vivant') which could already be heard in the phrase 'simplex in vitalitate' can then perhaps legitimately be likened to Benjamin's ('bloßes Leben') from the essay 'Zur Kritik der Gewalt'. On the basis of a point of overlap (in which the 'âme' or monad of the animal coincides with 'Seele des Lebendigen', the 'soul of the living'),

---

19 *Leibniz's Monadology*, §12.

20 Walter Benjamin, 'Dostoevsky's *The Idiot*' in *Early Writings: 1910–1917* (Howard Eiland ed. and trans.) (Cambridge, MA: Harvard University Press, 2011), p. 277.

the two can therefore be combined according to the following framework: 'naked life'—as Benjamin explained—is prey to myth, law, and violence, just as the simple monad—as Leibniz has explained—can, for Cartesians, appear mortal and devoid of soul. But just as Cartesians ignored the hazy little perceptions that one is not conscious of, vulgarly mistaking them for death, and therefore did not recognize the soul in the state of the naked animal monad, so the mythical dominion of power does not recognize the soul of the living being and unduly separates a naked mortal life, on which it stakes its pretences and exerts all of its violence (whereas, as is known, 'pure' or 'divine' violence is for Benjamin the destroyer only of myth and law, not of the soul of the living). Now, at this intersection one also finds articulated the distinction between these two models. While Leibniz's soul is indeed endowed with sensation, that is with perception accompanied by memory, and turns from being 'impérissable' (imperishable) to 'immortelle' (immortal) in a proper and human sense only if memory is tied to the knowledge of causes and consequences according to reason, for Benjamin immortality is no longer tied to remembrance; on the contrary, as in the case of Prince Myshkin, 'the prince's loss of memory is [. . .] is a symbol of the unforgettable character of his life.'[21] And because in Leibniz memory is the middle term that binds the eternal to the immortal and makes the soul into a personality, in Benjamin's conception it is instead the immortality of the unforgettable that 'apparently plummets into the abyss of the self's memory' and belongs to the living individual before it belongs to every personal individuality. (Thus, in an opposite and corresponding way, in the famous case of the man incapable of forgetting studied by Alexander Luria, the unforgettable is a surface on which nothing, whether that be an experience or a notion, ever ceases to be remembered and no memory responds to causes or dictates consequences or becomes truly personal and one's own.

21 Benjamin, 'Dostoievsky's *The Idiot*', p. 278.

In the person without memory, in the ailing prince or in the young Meyer, in the emptiness (or in the extreme saturation) in which the biographic line disappears (or, as Luria teaches, loses itself in an inflation of memories) and around which all efforts concentrate themselves, what dominates is not the simple life of the biological organism. In that naked monad, in that confused sensation, only the soul of the living being reigns, extraneous to possession, unforgettable even if not remembered, a momentary gift that does not belong to the unity or continuity of the individual. And then even the disjointed or disintegrated personality of the idiot or of the religious somnambulist or of the hysterical young woman can shine through in its pure form, without duration, as a perfect person. What remains unknown and unappropriable by consciousness is indeed the body and the immortal nature of consciousness itself.

51. Well before Bergson and Egger, it was Gustav Theodor Fechner who was interested in reports and studies of conditions of extreme risk. In drowning incidents and in other states proximate to death he had recognized a spiritual illumination similar to the perfect clarity granted at the moment of true death, when man finally sees all that is within him almost, one might say, like in an animated panorama, or in other words 'not confined to one particular direction of his thoughts, but looking into every direction at once'.[22] If for Fechner death is the door that is finally opened out onto the pure life of the spirit or the superior state of eternal wakefulness, existing beyond the limits of sensibility and corporeal finitude, it is first and foremost a condition at which man arrives gradually, passing from the stage of embryonic darkness through the phases of corporeal life, in which lucidity alternates with sleep. What therefore becomes decisive for the coherence of this framework is that the spirit is also aware of this path towards supreme clarity: hence the role of the brilliant intuition, of presentiment, or of moments of approximation during which, illuminating thus the continuity of the path, a

22 Gustav Theodor Fechner, *On Life After Death* (Hugo Wernekke trans.) (Chicago: Open Court Publishing Co., 1906), p. 77.

crack (*Spalte*) opens up in the door that is still closed, through which we see the dead, who in the meantime come alive for us.

'Why should you be afraid of the apparitions of spirits if you are not afraid of the figures of memory within you, which are the same thing?' More than a century had to pass since Fechner thus associated the afterlife with memory, and life as well as the presence of the dead with their recollection, for Alfred Döblin to turn this same theme via a wondrous evolution into the most comic and serious of parodies. In the novella *Reiseverkehr mit dem Jenseits* (1948), the finding of a corpse in apparently inexplicable circumstances provokes the intervention of a *medium*, and thence the morbid behaviour (*krankhaftes Wesen*) of certain spirits who, looking out onto 'the kingdom beyond death', gain access to the 'kingdom below death'. The outcome is transformed by Döblin's amusing prose into a less-than-numinous stylistic downgrade: those who have overcome the fatal border consider the descent among human beings to be a most vulgar act and believe that any contact with that inferior domain must be strenuously avoided. Never was prudence more justified. Although Fechner did not foresee it, it will in fact be enough for the weakest of them to be attracted to the threshold of the world down there for an entire crowd to line up behind him: news spreads fast, curiosity overcomes *politesse* and becomes intrusiveness. The by-now impatient souls do away with delays and open up through the small passageway offered by the *medium* new lines of communication (or continuity) between themselves and our world. Traffic (*Reiseverkehr*) thereby augments, and becomes ungovernable. Of course, there is nothing here, from the initial grotesque appearance of the lifeless body to the celestial evocations and happenings of his spirit that is not written in the most blatantly farcical tone; but when the reader—and only he, despite the still-credulous characters—discovers that the séances were a trick orchestrated by the two protagonists (the *medium* and the *soubrette*) to conceal their part in that strange death, then, instead of ending, the machinations and the farce transform: if the mask of the sensible is revealed as being deceiving and false, the seemingly caricatural content of the depiction, or better yet the collection of data obtained from the sessions, reveals an obstinate plausibility (so as to render the lie possible and for some even long-lasting). Of course, the entire story takes place in a burlesque key, but what is especially ironic is that the resolution of the detective story produces in exchange a theory or a truthful hypothesis concerning the existence of spirits, originating from their own stories. It affirms that in a man who is in a state of somnambular *trance* (or of *dépersonnalisation*) and is forgetful of himself, the voices of the afterlife speak, that is of those who live in that superior world because—as they say to the *medium*—they have not kept any memory of their earthly lives: this total forgetting has made them into a-biographical beings, untied from everything, and therefore immemorial and immortal. Perfectly contrary to what Fechner asserted, memory and survival are so radically distinct (both in the *medium* and in the spirit) that, according to a paradox that is only apparent, what survives of the person is the impersonal, the un-rememberable, that is to say, the non-individual. And if the voices of the afterlife speak through the voice of the clairvoyant, as soon as the trick is discovered once we realize that he is merely a common trickster, we end up understanding that he has never known anything about that which cannot be known or, in other words, that he has known the unknowable without being unable to know it, and that the invention of a world which by definition has no contact with reality can be not only an invention but an objective report . . . fiction cannot merely be called fiction, the theory of spiritism can appear both fantastical and incontrovertible. The voices themselves thus truly begin to gather and blend with ours. And it is only for this reason that in the face of an aware reader the characters can tranquilly keep believing: for indeed one cannot say that the mask of the trickster has entirely fallen, just as one cannot say that it has not multiplied by covering our faces, unbeknownst to us. The discovery is limited to the backstory—it cannot touch the immemorial and it cannot destroy like a castle of cards the world out there, to which the *medium* alluded; instead, it recognizes in the partition that separates the living from the dead the connection between substance and disguise, seriousness and pantomime, thus only putting an end to the exploitable nature of the lie.

Closing the *Petite histoire de la communion des vivants avec les morts* (1951), Georges Buraud had to pay homage to Frederic W. H. Myers and to his posthumous work, *Human Personality and Its Survival of Bodily Death* (1903), calling it 'the broadest and most profound synthesis of the facts of metapsychosis',[23] as important as the research of Niels Bohr and Max Planck in the domain of microphysics. Against the popular belief according to which a spirit is a dead individual authorized by providence to communicate with the living, Myers' theory of phantasms excludes the identity of the spectre and of the defunct individual ('Whatever [. . .] that phantom *was* [. . .] we cannot say that it was *himself* [. . .] the deceased person himself—a *revenant* coming back amongst the living men'),[24] to affirm instead that the former is a '*manifestation of persistent personal energy*'[25] now untied from intention and will, and that the dead individual is the cause of the apparition but not the person who appears. It is in other words 'possible that this force or influence, which after a man's death creates a phantasmal impression of him, may indicate no continuing action on his part, but may be some residue of the force or energy which he generated while yet alive'.[26]

It is precisely with death, that is, with the collapse of physical resistance, that force reveals its residual aspect, destined to impress itself via hallucinatory, telepathic or subliminal means on other bodies and individuals. The vitality of phantasmagorical appearances and of 'veridical after-images' can be attributed to the energetic economy, to the crises of effort (to use Pierre Janet's terms: of 'faiblesse' [weakness] or of 'force psychologique' [psychological force]), to its depressions (the 'misère psychologique' [psychological impoverishment]), to its balances or inflations; in other words, once again, to the superiority of consciousness with respect to the body. In Bergson's terms: if we 'regard the mental life

23 Georges Buraud, 'Petite histoire de la communion des vivants avec les morts' in Robert Aron and Jean-Claude Renard (eds), *Mors et vita* (Paris: Plon, 1951), p. 74.

24 Frederic W. H. Myers, *Human Personality and Its Survival of Bodily Death*, VOL. 2 (London: Longmans, Green and Co., 1903), p. 3.

25 Myers, *Human Personality*, p. 4.

26 Myers, *Human Personality*, p. 4.

as much more vast than the cerebral life, survival becomes so probable that the burden of proof comes to lie on him who denies it rather than on him who affirms it'; 'the more we become accustomed to this idea of a consciousness overflowing the organism, the more natural we find it to suppose that the soul survives the body'.[27] The basilical power of the former over the latter thus extends itself via an economy of spectres that is both—Bergson's last phrase can also be inverted—at the origin of that power and that maintains it by transforming it into something spontaneous, rendering it habitual.

Or perhaps not. Perhaps we could imagine a development different from Myers's hypothesis, one which might truly separate it from the principle of individuality, from the domain of the voluntary and involuntary, from finality and intention, yes, and even before that from causality. To conceive of the phantasm, or of so-called memory, as a pure, unmotivated effect, we would have to imagine it as having no relation to the prior living being, or in other words, we—we who are enclosed in the uncontested and deadly domain of images—would have to think an image without death or a survival that is not merely posthumous. If spirits live and live in us, if they lose their memory and become immortal, we might say it is because the immortal or the unforgettable is not merely a forgetfulness of the self or of the imminent end. The phenomenon would then lose its paranormal exceptionality, since it would originate not in a residual force, unexhausted by death, but in a pure absence of effort. And this is not the *détente* of the instant proximate to the end that imprints its exemplary character onto all of existence. Rather, it is in that which we love, and therefore think of without knowing it, in the heedless gesture or glance, in every loss, in every missed opportunity like in the unnoticed breath, in everything that remains below the threshold of your habitual vigilance, that immortal life shines. And death is not the extreme possibility in which a suffering body clings to intelligence or in which instead 'la conscience qui déborde l'organisme' (consciousness that extends beyond the organism) appears, but is rather both an exit

27 Henri Bergson, 'Phantasms of the Living and Psychical Research' in *Mind-Energy*, pp. 78–79.

from the corporeal prison and from the body's awareness and mastery, that is, a moment amongst others, of apparent loss or distraction, in which the soul of the living still shines, untouched, with its little perceptions. Consciousness—as Husserl would say—is always vigilant; and there is no loss or death because consciousness—despite Husserl—is not an adherence and possession and grasping of the self: it is pure, that much is true, and also disinterested, but this trait is not caused in turn by an 'interest in disinterestedness', since much like Döblin's spirits it neither knows nor respects identity. The break between the actual and the in-actual, the 'non positional' and the reflected, living and past consciousness, thought and body (wakefulness and sleep, reason and folly) is only necessarily and functional to the principle of property and masterly unity, and it must be continuously recomposed—against a different conception of having (whether Tardian or genuinely Leibnizian)—only so that it can affirm itself. Something, however—beyond the barrier and precisely here, in a specular alterity, in an afterlife that is absolute unreality or reality itself—eludes one's grasp, and thus every grasp eludes the I: consciousness, that same immediate consciousness of the self, is only immortal and forgetful of itself, it does not sediment itself in a substrate, does not remain tied to reflexive identity but is illuminated in a temporality that belongs to no one. The imperious and suggestive voice of the body, that speaks in the silences of illness and pins down and holds back the spirit, oppressing and covering it ('Nobody has perhaps ever had a more fitting constitution that mine,' Biran wrote in 1818, 'to recognize the subordination of the moral state to the physical one') is nothing other than the organic force (an excess of resistance corresponding to the *surplus* of spiritual force liberated by death) that affirms itself over the lucidity of the I, traversing it like the voice of a ventriloquist. But wherever this force truly disappears and resistance renounces its pretensions, the object and antagonist of the basilical power also ceases to appear as merely organic and unaware life, and reveals itself for what it is: the otherwise suffocated and rebellious life of the living, or even of 'consciousness' itself. Wherever this force disappears, nobody dies and in anyone and in every lack everyone lives, and everything is conscious of itself, because the true *petites perceptions* escape us, now, like in the final panorama, and do not belong to anyone. Everything is equally 'confused' and indeterminable, and the most whirling vertigo (that captures the subject identical to himself and makes him suffer) is the happy condition of multiplications, in which individuality itself disperses in the process of living.

52. The affirmation of identity coincides with the projection of death that imposes both the alternative and the order: the 'first' or 'second' existence, active or passive. For this reason, the I and only the I is the ever-threatened and frightened owner. And only the mask of the dead man ties the body to the mask and the person to the body. To defeat its dominion, to loosen the bond or avoid the effort, this double action that separates and holds together, truly means emancipating existence from duration and from fateful moments, eliminating ecstasy in concentration and concentration in ecstasy, enacting true relaxation by affirming distracted attention or consciousness without limits everywhere . . . Every effort disappears here, because beyond effort there is no spirit or talking corpse . . . nobody dies. And there is no true alternative between the instantaneity of the *cogito* and duration, between the actuality of the present and the flow of time and thought.

A much-overlooked philosopher wrote, 'we know this refrain of dominating melancholy: Where is the snow of old? Indeed, according to common understanding, past time is that which no longer is. A mistake! It is, on the contrary, reality in its most concrete aspect, it is the indestructible. Time past is what it is . . . '[28]

We are not made of thought, or of flesh and blood . . . we are made of the past, and the past does not belong to us and that which does not belong to us is unforgettable.

---

28 Joseph Delboeuf, 'Le sommeil et les rêves, considérés principalement dans leurs rapports avec les théories de la certitude et de la mémoire (le principe de la fixation de la force)' in *Le sommeil et les rêves: Le magnétisme animal. Quelques considérations sur la psychologie de l'hypnotisme* (Paris: Fayard, 1993[1885]), p. 247.

... There is no identity and therefore no doubleness of the subject, merely the amphiboly of a force that splits, in resisting, into possession and possessor and in that same undue scission remains one and calls itself power, projecting itself onto a mythical continuity. What dominates here is the appearance of personality, which can be put on by one or another only because its abstract and general sense coincides with the brutal one of chance. This mask, defined by historically conditioned relations of force 'does not just exist with its feet on the ground' but, as was the case in Vienna at the beginning of 1825, it can stand on its head before others, evolving out of its wooden brain grotesque ideas, far more wonderful than 'table-turning' ever was ...

Only a random state of consciousness (appropriation itself does not escape this law) can truly be, in its peculiar, unaware brevity, a past: *and precisely that past with which instantaneity itself has burnt all bridges, which no longer belongs to it because it never could have. Or, more precisely—as Gustav Landauer has written—*'Everything that happens, no matter where and when, is the past; *not an effect of the past, but the past itself*';[29] *so that every day—as another brilliant reader glossed—'like sleepers, we use unmeasured energies. What we do and think is filled with the being of our father and ancestors'.*[30] *And every thought or glance possesses an inadvertent and anonymous aspect, 'not owned', incognito and eternal: it is a 'perfect person'—that is all that can be said and only as a hypothesis. Indeed, 'all we can know is this: our life does not run its course for the fashions and struggles of the day, but for that which is unknown, buried in the depths and unexpected ...'*[31]

---

29 Gustav Landauer, *Revolution and Other Political Writings: A Political Reader* (Gabriel Kuhn ed. and trans.) (Oakland, CA: PM Press, 2010), p. 122.

30 Walter Benjamin, 'The Metaphysics of Youth' in *Early Writings: 1910–1917*, p. 144.

31 Landauer, *Die Revolution*, p. 119.

Bibliography

ABBÉ DE LIGNAC. *Le témoignage du sens intime et de l'expérience*. Auxerre: Fournier, 1760.

ADORNO, Theodor W. 'Gloss on Personality' in *Critical Models: Interventions and Catchwords* (Henry W. Pickford trans.). New York, NY: Columbia University Press, 2005.

ALQUIÉ, Ferdinand. *Leçons sur Descartes: Science et métaphysique chez Descartes*. Paris: La Table Ronde, 2005.

ANSARI, Keath, and John Mullarkey (eds). *Henri Bergson: Key Writings*. New York, NY: Continuum, 2002.

ARISTOTLE. *De sensu* in *De sensu and De memoria* (G. R. T. Ross trans.). Cambridge: Cambridge University Press, 1906.

AZAM, Étienne Eugène. 'Amnésie périodique, ou doublement de la vie'. *Revue scientifique* 2(5) (1876).

AZAM, Étienne Eugène. *Hypnotisme, double conscience et altérations de la personnalité* (J.-M. Charcot pref. and Serge Nicholas intro.). Paris: L'Harmattan, 2004[1887].

AZOUVI, François (ed.). *Mémoire sur la décomposition de la pensée précédé du Mémoire sur les rapports de l'idéologie et des mathématiques, Œuvres de Maine de Biran*, VOL. 3. Paris: Vrin, 2000[1804].

AZOUVI, François (ed.). *Nouvelles considérations sur le sommeil, les songes et le somnambulisme* in *Discours à la société médicale de Bergerac, Œuvres de Maine de Biran*, VOL. 5. Paris: Vrin, 1984[1809].

AZOUVI, François. *Maine de Biran: La science de l'homme*. Paris: Vrin, 1995.

BACHELARD, Gaston. *The Dialectic of Duration* (Mary McAllester Jones trans.). London: Rowman and Littlefield, 2016.

BACHELARD, Gaston. *Intuition of the Instant* (Eileen Rizo-Patron trans.). Evanston, IL: Northwestern University Press, 2013.

BAERTSCHI, Bernard (ed.). *Conversation avec MM. Degérando et Ampère* in *Rapports des sciences naturelles avec la psychologie et autres écrits sur la psychologie, Œuvres de Maine de Biran*, VOL. 8. Paris: Vrin, 1986[1813].

BAERTSCHI, Bernard (ed.). *Extrait de Reil (De organo animæ)* in *Nouvelles considérations sur les rapports du physique et du moral. Textes relatifs à la physiologie autour de 1820, Œuvres de Maine de Biran*, VOL. 9. Paris: Vrin, 1990[1820].

BAERTSCHI, Bernard (ed.). *Note sur un passage très-remarquable du Teimognage du sens intime par l'abbé de Lignac (1815)* in *Commentaires et marginalia: XVIIIe siècle, Œuvres de Maine de Biran*, VOL. 11, PART 2. Paris: Vrin, 1993[1815].

BAERTSCHI, Bernard (ed.). *Nouveaux essais d'anthropologie* in *Dernière philosophie. Existence et anthropologie. Nouveaux essais d'anthropologie. Notes sur l'idée d'existence, Œuvres de Maine de Biran*, VOL. 10, PART 2. Paris: Vrin, 1989[1823–1824].

BAERTSCHI, Bernard (ed.). *Nouvelles considérations sur les rapports du physique et du moral de l'homme (1820)* in *Nouvelles considérations sur les rapports du physique et du moral. Textes relatifs à la physiologie autour de 1820, Œuvres de Maine de Biran*, VOL. 9. Paris: Vrin, 1990[1820].

BALL, Benjamin. *Leçons sur les maladies mentales*. Paris: Asselin et Houzeau, 1890.

BARTHEZ, Paul-Joseph. *Nouveau éléments de la science de l'homme*, VOL. 1. Montpellier: Jean Martel, the Elder, 1578.

BENJAMIN, Walter. *Early Writings: 1910–1917* (Howard Eiland ed. and trans.). Cambridge, MA: Harvard University Press, 2011.

BERARD, Frédéric. *Doctrine des rapports du physique et du moral: Pour servir de fondement à la métaphysique, à la physiologie dite intellectuelle et à la métaphysique*. Paris: Gabon et Compagnie, 1823.

BERGSON, Henri. *Creative Evolution* (Arthur Mitchell trans.). Mineola, NY: Dover Publications, Inc., 1998.

BERGSON, Henri. *Écrits philosophiques* (Arnaud Bouaniche, François, Élie During, Frédéric Fruteau de Laclos, Frédéric Keck, Stéphane Madelrieux, Camille Riquier, Ghislain Waterlot and Frédéric Worms eds). Paris: Presses Universitaires de France, 2001[1891].

BERGSON, Henri. *Essai sur les données immédiates de la conscience*. Paris: Presses Universitaires de France, 1948[1889].

BERGSON, Henri. *An Introduction to Metaphysics* (T. E. Hulme trans., John Mullarkey and Michael Kolkman eds). New York: Macmillan, 1985.

BERGSON, Henri. *Matter and Memory* (N. M. Paul and W. S. Palmer trans). New York, NY: Zone Books, 1991.

BERGSON, Henri. *Mind-Energy: Lectures and Essays* (H. Wildon Carr trans.). London: Macmillan and Co., 1920.

BERNARD-LEROY, Eugène. *L'illusion de fausse reconnaissance*. Paris: Alcan, 1898.

BERNARD-LEROY, Eugène. 'Sur l'illusion dite "dépersonnalisation"'. *Revue Philosophique de la France et de l'Étranger* 46 (1898).

BLANCHOT, Maurice. *The Infinite Conversation* (Susan Hanson trans.). Minneapolis, MN: University of Minnesota Press, 1993.

BLANCHOT, Maurice. *L'espace littéraire*. Paris: Gallimard, 1955.

BLONDEL, Maurice. *Une énigme historique: Le 'Vinculum Substantiale' d'après Leibniz et l'ébauche d'un réalisme supérieur*. Paris: Beauchesne, 1930.

BOEHM, Alfred. *Le 'Vinculum substantiale' chez Leibniz: Ses origine historiques*. Paris: Vrin, 1938.

BONNET, Charles. *Essai analytique sur les facultés de l'âme*. Copenhagen: C. et A. Philibert, 1760.

BONNET, Charles. *La palingénésie philosophique ou Idées sur l'état passé et sur l'état futur des êtres vivants*. Geneva: Philibert et Chirol, 1769.

BOUANICHE, Arnaud, François, Élie During, Frédéric Fruteau de Laclos, Frédéric Keck, Stéphane Madelrieux, Camille Riquier, Ghislain Waterlot and Frédéric Worms (eds). *Écrits philosophiques*. Paris: Presses Universitaires de France, 2001[1891].

BRÉHIER, Émile. *The Nineteenth Century: Period of Systems (1800–1850), The History of Philosophy*, VOL. 6 (Wade Baskin trans.). Chicago, IL: University of Chicago Press, 1968.

BRÉHIER, Émile. 'Une forme archaïque du cogito ergo sum'. *Revue Philosophique de la France et de l'Étranger* 133(10–12) (1942–1943).

BRUNSCHVICG, Léon. 'La pensée intuitive chez Descartes et chez les cartésiens' in *Écrits philosophiques*, VOL. 1. Paris: Presses Universitaires de France, 1951[1927].

BRUNSCHVICG, Léon. *René Descartes*. Paris: Redier, 1937.

BURAUD, Georges. 'Petite histoire de la communion des vivants avec les morts' in Robert Aron and Jean-Claude Renard (eds), *Mors et vita*. Paris: Plon, 1951.

CABANIS, Pierre-Jean-Georges. *Rapports du physique et du moral de l'homme*, 2nd EDN., VOL. 1. Paris: Crapart, Caille et Ravier, 1805[1802].

CANGUILHEM, Georges. *Knowledge of Life* (Paola Marrati and Todd Meyers eds, Stefanos Geroulanos and Daniela Ginsburg trans.). New York, NY: Fordham University Press, 2008.

CHITUSSI, Barbara. *Lo spettacolo di sé: Filosofia della doppia personalità*. Milan: Meltemi, 2018.

DELBOEUF, Joseph. 'Le sommeil et les rêves, considérés principalement dans leurs rapports avec les théories de la certitude et de la mémoire (le principe de la fixation de la force)' in *Le sommeil et les rêves: Le magnétisme animal. Quelques considérations sur la psychologie de l'hypnotisme*. Paris: Fayard, 1993[1885].

DELEUZE, Gilles. *The Fold: Leibniz and the Baroque* (Tom Conley trans.). Minneapolis: University of Minnesota Press, 1993.

DEONNA, Waldemar. 'Un art nouveau: Le tactilisme'. *Journal de psychologie normale et pathologique* 20(1) (1923).

DERRIDA, Jacques. 'Cogito and the History of Madness' in *Writing and Difference* (Alan Bass trans.). Chicago, IL: Chicago University Press, 1978.

DERRIDA, Jacques. *Voice and Phenomenon: Introduction to the Problem of the Sign in Husserl's Phenomenology* (Leonard Lawlor trans.). Evanston, IL: Northwestern University Press, 2011.

DESCARTES, René. *Discours de la méthode* (Étienne Gilson ed.). Paris: Vrin, 1962[1637].

DESTUTT DE TRACY, Antoine-Louis-Claude. *Éléments d'Idéologie*, VOL. 1: *De l'Idéologie proprement dite*. Paris: Courcier, 1817[1801].

DEVARIEUX, Anne. 'L'exil des affections pures: À propos d'une formule d'Ovide et de sa reprise biranienne'. *Revue philosophique de Louvain* 103(1–2) (2005).

DREYFUS, Ginette. 'Discussion sur le "Cogito" et l'axiome "Pour penser il faut être"'. *Revue Internationale de Philosophie* 6(19) (1952).

DURKHEIM, Emile. 'The Dualism of Human Nature and its Social Conditions' in Kurt Wolff (ed.), *Essays on Sociology and Philosophy*. New York, NY: Harper & Row, 1964.

DURKHEIM, Émile. *The Elementary Forms of the Religious Life* (Joseph Ward Swain trans.). London: George Allen & Unwin Ltd, 1964.

EGGER, Victor. 'Le moi des mourants. Nouveaux faits'. *Revue Philosophique de la France et de l'Étranger* 42 (1896).

FECHNER, Gustav Theodor. *On Life After Death* (Hugo Wernekke trans.). Chicago: Open Court Publishing Co., 1906.

FOUCAULT, Michel. *The Birth of the Clinic: An Archaeology of Medical Perception* (A. M. Sheridan Smith trans.). New York: Random House, 1973.

FOUILLÉE, Alfred. *Descartes*. Paris: Hachette, 1893.

FOUILLÉE, Alfred. *La pensée et les nouvelles écoles anti-intellectualistes*. Paris: Alcan, 1911.

FOUILLÉE, Alfred. *La psychologie des idées-forces*, VOL. 1. Paris: Alcan, 1893.

FRANK, Joseph. *Traité de pathologie interne*, VOL. 2. Brussels: Société Encyclographique, 1842.

FRÉMONT, Christiane (ed.). *Commentaire sur les Méditations métaphysiques de Descartes (1813)* in *Commentaires et marginalia: XVIIe siècle, Œuvres de Maine de Biran*, VOL. 11, PART 1. Paris: Vrin, 1990[1813].

FUNKE, Gerhard. *Maine de Biran: Philosophisches und politisches Denken zwischen Ancien Régime und Bürgerkönigtum in Frankreich*. Bonn: H. Bouvier, 1947.

GANUALT, Joël (ed.). *Notes sur le Premier Problème de la Philosophie* in *Commentaires et marginalia: XIXe siècle, Œuvres de Maine de Biran*, VOL. 11, PART 3. Paris: Vrin, 1990[1813–1815].

GERHARDT, Carl Immanuel (ed.). *Die philosophische Schriften von Gottfried Wilhelm Leibniz*, VOL. 7. Hildesheim: Georg Olms, 1996[1710].

GILLES DE LA TOURETTE, Georges. *L'hypnotisme et les états analogues au point de vue médico-légal* (Paul Brouardel pref.). Paris: E. Plon, 1887.

GOUGHIER, Henri. *Les conversions de Maine de Biran*. Paris: Vrin, 1948.

GOUHIER, Henri (ed.). *Journal*, VOL. 1: *Février 1814–31 décembre 1816*. Neuchâtel: Éditions la Baconnière, 1954.

GOUHIER, Henri (ed.). *Journal*, VOL. 2: *1er janvier 1817–17 mai 1824*. Neuchâtel: Éditions la Baconnière, 1955.

GOUHIER, Henri (ed.). *Journal*, VOL. 3: *Agendas, carnets et notes*. Neuchâtel: Éditions la Baconnière, 1957.

GOUHIER, Henri. 'Maine de Biran et Bergson' in *Études sur l'histoire des idées en France depuis le XVIIe siècle*. Paris: Vrin, 1980[1948].

GUYAU, Jean-Marie. *La genèse de l'idée de temps* (Alfred Fouillée intro.). Paris: Alcan, 1890.

HEIDEGGER, Martin. *Being and Time* (Joan Stambaugh trans.). New York, NY: State University of New York Press, 1996.

HEIDEGGER, Martin. *Nihilism* (Frank A. Capuzzi trans., David Farrell Krell ed.), *Nietzsche*, VOL. 4. San Francisco, CA: Harper & Row, 1979.

HELLER-ROAZEN, Daniel. *The Inner Touch: Archaeology of a Sensation*. New York: Zone Books, 2007.

HENRY, Michel. *Philosophie et phénoménologie du corps: Essai sur l'ontologie biranienne*. Paris: Presses Universitaires de France, 1965.

HORKHEIMER, Max. 'On Bergson's Metaphysics of Time' (Peter Thomas trans.). *Radical Philosophy* 131 (2005).

HUSSERL, Edmund. *The Paris Lectures* (Peter Koestenbaum trans.). Dordrecht: Kluwer Academic Publishers, 1998.

HUSSERL, Edmund. *Zur Phänomenologie der Intersubjektivität. Texte aus dem Nachlass*, VOL. 3: 1929–1935, *Husserliana*, VOL. 15 (Iso Kern ed.). The Hague: Njihoff, 1973.

JAMES, William. 'Person and Personality: From Johnson's Universal Cyclopaedia' in *Essays in Psychology*. Cambridge, MA: Harvard University Press, 1983[1895].

JANET, Paul. 'La notion de personnalité'. *Revue scientifique*, 2nd EDN, 10(50) (1876).

JANET, Pierre. *De l'angoisse à l'extase: Études sur les croyances et les sentiments*, VOL. 2: *Les sentiments fondamentaux*. Paris: Félix Alcan, 1928.

JANET, Pierre. *L'évolution psychologique de la personnalité: Compte-rendu intégral des conférences d'après les notes sténographiques* (Miron Epstein ed.). Paris: Chahine, 1929.

JANET, Pierre. *Les obsessions et la psychasthénie*, VOL. 1. Paris: Félix Alcan, 1903.

JESI, Furio. *Bachofen* (Andrea Cavalletti ed.). Turin: Bollati Boringhieri, 2005.

KRISHABER, Maurice. *De la névropathie cérébro-cardique*. Paris: Masson, 1873.

LANDUAER, Gustav. *Revolution and Other Political Writings: A Political Reader* (Gabriel Kuhn ed. and trans.). Oakland, CA: PM Press, 2010.

LEIBNIZ, Gottfried Wilhelm. *Discourse on Metaphysics and Other Writings* (Peter Lopston ed.). Buffalo, NY: Broadview Press, 2012.

LEIBNIZ, Gottfried Wilhelm. *Leibniz's Monadology: A New Translation And Guide* (Lloyd Strickland trans.). Edinburgh: Edinburgh University Press, 2014.

LEIBNIZ, Gottfried Wilhelm. *New Essays on Human Understanding* (Peter Remnant and Jonathan Bennett eds and trans). Cambridge: Cambridge University Press, 1996.

LEIBNIZ, Gottfried Wilhelm. *Principes de la nature et de la grâce fondés en raison* (André Robinet ed.). Paris: Presses Universitaires de France, 2002.

LEIBNIZ, Gottfried Wilhelm. *Theodicy: Essays on the Goodness of God and the Freedom of Man and the Origin of Evil* (E. M. Huggard trans.). New Haven, CT: Yale University Press, 1952.

LINN, Sidney E. 'Poe and Mesmerism'. *PMLA* 62 (1947).

MAIMON, Solomon. *The Autobiography of Solomon Maimon* (Yitzhak Y. Melamed and Abraham Socher eds, Paul Reitter trans.). Princeton, NJ: Princeton University Press, 2018.

MAINE DE BIRAN, Marie-François-Pierre Gonthier. *Of Immediate Apperception* (Mark Sinclair trans., Alessandro Aloisi and Marco Piazza intrs). London: Bloomsbury Academic, 2020.

MARQUARD, Odo. *Apologie des Zufälligen: Philosophische Studien*. Stuttgart: Reclam, 1996[1986].

MARX, Karl. *Capital*, VOL. 3. London: Electric Book Co., 2001.

MARX, Karl. 'Saint Max' in *The German Ideology*, VOL. 1. Amherst, NY: Prometheus, 1998.

MERLEAU-PONTY, Maurice. *The Incarnate Subject: Malebranche, Biran and Bergson on the Union of Body and Soul* (Jacques Taminiaux pref., Paul B. Milan trans.,

Andre G. Bjelland Jr. and Patrick Burke eds). Amherst, NY: Humanity Books, 2001.

MICHAUX, Henri. *Les commencements: Dessins d'enfants, essais d'enfant*. Montpellier: Fata Morgana, 1983.

MINKOWSKI, Eugène. *La schizophrénie: Psychopathologie des schizoïdes et des schizophrènes* (Sven Follin pref.). Paris: Payot, 1997[1927].

MINKOWSKI, Eugène. *Lived Time* (Nancy Metzel trans.). Evanston, IL: Northwestern University Press, 1970.

MOMIGLIANO, Arnaldo. *Lo sviluppo della biografia greca*. Turin: Einaudi, 1974.

MOREAU DE TOURS, Jacques-Joseph. 'De l'identité de l'état de rêve et de la folie'. *Annales médico-psychologiques* 3(1) (1855).

MOREAU DE TOURS, Jacques-Joseph (Moreau de Tours). *Hasish and Mental Illness* (Hélène Peters and Gabriel G. Nahas eds, Gordon J. Barnett trans.). New York: Raven Press, 1973.

MYERS, Frederic W. H. *Human Personality and Its Survival of Bodily Death*, VOL. 2. London: Longmans, Green and Co., 1903.

NANCY, Jean-Luc. *Ego sum: Corpus, Anima, Fabula* (Marie-Eve Morin trans.). New York, NY: Fordham University Press, 2016.

PATOČKA, Jan. *Die Bewegung der menschlichen Existenz: Phänomenologische Schriften II* (Klaus Nellen, Jiří Němec and Ilja Srubar eds). Stuttgart: Klett-Cotta, 1991.

PEREZ, Bernard. 'Le caractère et les mouvements'. *Revue Philosophique de la France et de l'Étranger* 31 (1891).

POULET, Georges. 'Bergson: Le thème de la vision panoramique des mourants et la juxtaposition' in *L'espace proustien*. Paris: Gallimard, 1982[1963].

RAVAISSON, Félix. *De l'habitude*. Paris: Fayard, 1984[1838].

RAVAISSON, Félix. *Of Habit* (Clare Carlisle and Mark Sinclair trans). London: Continuum, 2008.

RENOUVIER, Charles. *Le personnalisme, suivi d'une Étude sur la perception externe et sur la force*. Paris: Alcan, 1903.

RENOUVIER, Charles. *Traité de psychologie rationnelle d'après les principes du criticisme*, VOL. 1, *Essais de critique générale*, VOL. 2. Paris: Colin, 1912.

RIBOT, Théodule. *Les maladies de la personnalité*. Paris: Alcan, 1883.

RICOEUR, Paul. *À l'école de la phénoménologie*. Paris: Vrin, 2004[1986].

SARTRE, Jean-Paul. *The Transcendence of the Ego: A Sketch for a Phenomenological Description* (Andre Brown trans.). London: Routledge, 2004.

SCHMITT, Carl. *Political Romanticism* (Guy Oakes trans.). Cambridge, MA: MIT Press, 1986.

SIDIS, Boris, and Simon P. Goodhart. *Multiple Personality: An Experimental Investigation into the Nature of Human Individuality*. New York: D. Appleton and Company, 1905.

SIDIS, Boris. *Philistine and Genius*, 2nd EDN. Boston: Richard G. Badger, 1917.

SIDIS, Boris. *The Psychology of Laughter*. New York: D. Appleton and Company, 1913.

SIDIS, Boris. *The Psychology of Suggestion: A Research into the Subconscious Nature of Man and Society* (William James intro.). New York: D. Appleton and Company, 1903.

SIDIS, William Hames. 'Unconscious Intelligence' in Boris Sidis, *Symptomatology, Psychognosis, and Diagnosis of Psychopathic Diseases*. Boston: Richard G. Badger, 1914.

SIMONDON, Gilbert. *Individuation in Light of Notions of Form and Information* (Taylor Adkins trans.). Minneapolis: University of Minnesota Press, 2020.

SOURIAU, Étienne. *Les différent modes d'existence*. Paris: Presses Universitaires de France, 1943.

SOURIAU, Étienne. *The Different Modes of Existence* (Erik Beranek and Tim Howles trans). Minneapolis, MN: Univocal, 2015.

SPINOZA, Baruch. *Treatise on the Correction of the Intellect* in *Ethics and Treatise on the Correction of the Intellect* (Andrew Boyle trans.). London: J. M. Dent., 1993.

SPITZER, Leo. *Stilstudien*, VOL. 2: *Stilsprachen*. Munich: Hueber, 1928.

STAROBINSKI, Jean. *Action and Reaction: The Life and Adventures of a Couple* (Sophie Hawkes and Jeff Fort trans). New York, NY: Zone Books, 2003.

STIRNER, Max. *The Ego and Its Own* (David Leopold trans.). Cambridge: Cambridge University Press, 1995.

TAINE, Hippolyte. *On Intelligence* (Daniel N. Robinson ed.). Washington, DC: University Publications of America, 1977.

TAINE, Hippolyte. 'Sur les éléments et sur la formation de l'idée du moi'. *Revue Philosophique de la France et de l'Étranger* 1 (1876).

TARDE, Gabriel. *Maine de Biran et l'évolutionnisme en psychologie* (Éric Alliez fore. and Anne Devarieux pref.). Paris: Institut d'édition Sanofi-Synthélabo, 2000[1876].

TARDE, Gabriel. *Monadologie et sociologie*, *Œuvres de Gabriel Tarde*, VOL. 1 (Éric Alliez pres. and Maurizio Lazzarato postf.). Le Plessis-Robinson: Institut Synthélabo pour le progrès de la connaissance, 1999[1893].

TARDE, Gabriel. 'Qu'est-ce qu'une société?'. *Revue Philosophique de la France et de l'Étranger* 18 (1884).

THIBAUDET, Albert. *Trente ans de vie française, Le Bergsonisme*, VOL. 3. Paris: Gallimard, 1924[1923].

TILLIETTE, Xavier. 'Nouvelles réflexions sur le Cogito biranien'. *Revue de Métaphysique et de Morale* 88(4) (1983).

VALÉRY, Paul. 'A View of Descartes' in *Collected Works of Paul Valéry*, VOL. 9: *Masters and Friends* (Martin Turnell trans.). Princeton, NJ: Princeton University Press, 1968.

WAHL, Jean André. *Du rôle de l'idée de l'instant dans la philosophie de Descartes.* Paris: Vrin, 1953[1920].

WAHL, Jean. *Husserl.* Paris: Centre de Documentation Universitaire, 1958.

WAHL, Jean. *Tableau de la philosophie française.* Paris: Fontaine, 1946.

WINSLOW, Forbes. *Obscure Diseases of the Brain and Mind.* Philadelphia: Lea, 1866[1860].